A Plethora of Polyhedra
in Origami

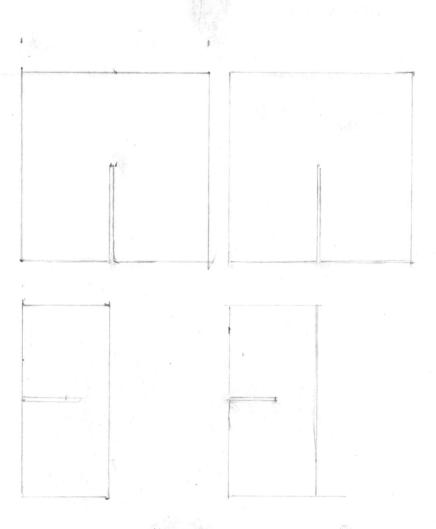

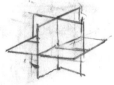

Other books by John Montroll:

Origami Sculptures

Prehistoric Origami *Dinosaurs and Other Creatures*

Origami Sea Life by John Montroll and Robert J. Lang

African Animals in Origami

Origami Inside-Out

North American Animals in Origami

Mythological Creatures and the Chinese Zodiac in Origami

Teach Yourself Origami

Bringing Origami to Life

Dollar Bill Animals in Origami

Bugs and Birds in Origami

Animal Origami for the Enthusiast

Origami for the Enthusiast

Easy Origami

Birds in Origami

Favorite Animals in Origami

A Plethora of Polyhedra
in Origami

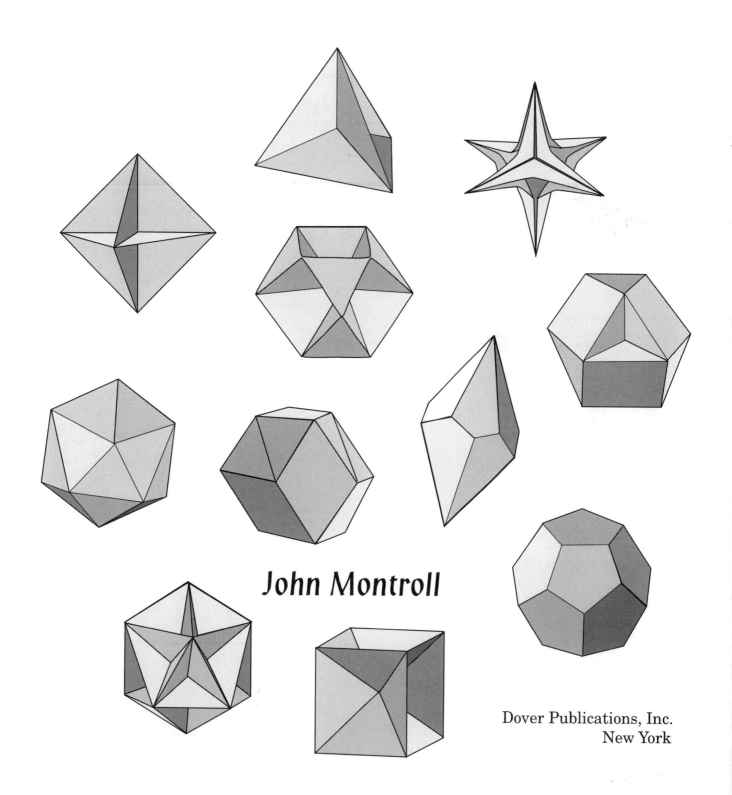

John Montroll

Dover Publications, Inc.
New York

To Max and Craig

Published in Canada by General Publishing Company, Ltd.,
895 Don Mills Road, 400-2 Park Centre, Toronto, Ontario M3C 1W3.
  Published in the United Kingdom by David & Charles, Brunel House,
Forde Close, Newton Abbot, Devon TQ12 4PU.

Bibliographical Note

This work is first published in 2002 in separate editions by
Antroll Publishing Company, Maryland, and Dover Publications,
Inc., New York.

Library of Congress Cataloging-in-Publication Data

Montroll, John.
    A plethora of polyhedra in origami : John Montroll.
        p. cm.
    ISBN 0-486-42271-2 (pbk.)
    1. Origami. 2.Polyhedra in art.   I. Title.
  TT870.M5726 2002
  736'.982—dc21

                                                              2001047905

Manufactured in the United States of America
  Dover Publications, Inc., 31 East 2nd Street, Mineola, N.Y. 11501

Introduction

olyhedra are some of the most beautiful geometric shapes imaginable. The ancient Greeks and other cultures believed polyhedra had mystical powers. Each shape seems to radiate a different feeling. In this collection you will make many discoveries as you uncover the secrets of folding polyhedra. It is very satisfying to create your own, each from a single square sheet of paper.

You will learn to fold the five Platonic solids—the tetrahedron, cube, octahedron, icosahedron, and dodecahedron. Also here are the sunken versions of these five shapes and several diamonds, prisms, heptahedron, six-pointed star, rhombic dodecahedron, and several other polyhedra.

Generally polyhedra are constructed from wood, plastic, stone, metal, or paper. From paper, the usual way is to either use multiple sheets or one which has been cut to a two-dimensional silhouette of the unfolded shape. In any of these methods, the polyhedron is as symmetric as the shape itself is, that is, all the sides are constructed in the same way. By the choice of using a single square, the polyhedra exhibit a different character—some sides are connected, some are locked or connected from the opposite side of the paper. The thicknesses of the sides are different. Inherent in this is that each shape carries an organic nature.

The models have been organized in groups of related polyhedra. Each group is ordered by level of difficulty, and each group itself becomes progressively more difficult. The illustrations conform to the internationally accepted Randlett-Yoshizawa conventions. The colored side of origami paper is represented by the shadings in the diagrams. Origami paper can be found in many hobby shops or purchased by mail from OrigamiUSA, 15 West 77th Street, New York, NY 10024-5192 or from Dover Publications, Inc., 31 East 2nd Street, Mineola, NY 11501. Large sheets are easier to use than small ones.

Many people helped make this origami polyhedra symphony possible. I thank George Hart and Peter Messer for their information on polyhedra. I thank Robert Lang for his efficeint folding sequences. Thanks to Russell Cashdollar for his continued support on this project. Thanks to Tom Slemmons for his ideas. Thanks to my editors, Jan Polish and Charley Montroll. Of course, I also thank the many folders who proof read the diagrams.

John Montroll

Contents

★   Simple
★★   Intermediate
★★★   Complex
★★★★   Very Complex

The Platonic Solids   *page 11*

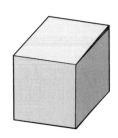

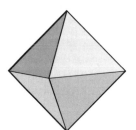

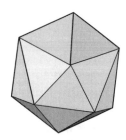

Tetrahedron
★
page 12

Cube
★★
page 14

Octahedron
★★
page 16

Icosahedron
★★★
page 18

Diamonds   *page 22*

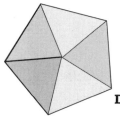

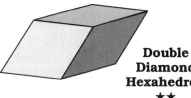

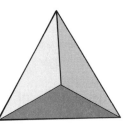

Decahedron
★★
page 23

Double Diamond Hexahedron
★★
page 25

Triangular Dipyramid
★★
page 27

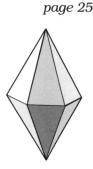

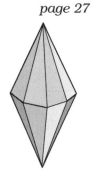

Pentagonal Dipyramid
★★
page 31

Hexagonal Dipyramid
★★
page 35

Heptagonal Dipyramid
★★
page 38

Prisms   *page 42*

Triangular Prism
★★
page 42

Pentagonal Prism
★★
page 45

Hexagonal Prism
★★
page 49

Based on the Octahedron *page 53* ───────────────

Six-Pointed Star
★★
page 54

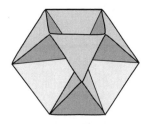

Octahemioctahedron
★★★
page 57

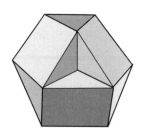

Cubehemioctahedron
★★★
page 60

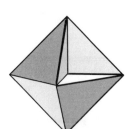

Heptahedron
★★★
page 63

Dimpled Octahedron
★★★
page 67

Sunken Platonic Solids ───────
page 71

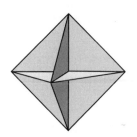

Sunken Octahedron
★★
page 72

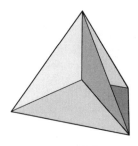

Sunken Tetrahedron
★★★
page 75

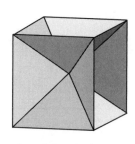

Sunken Cube
★★★
page 80

Sunken Dodecahedron
★★★★
page 85

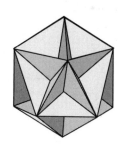

Sunken Icosahedron
★★★★
page 90

Dodecahedra *page 95* ───────────────

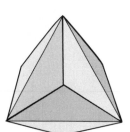

Triakis Tetrahedron
★★★
page 96

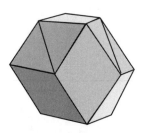

Rhombic Dodecahedron
★★★
page 100

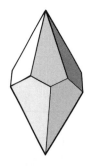

**Pentagonal
Trapezohedron**
★★★★
page 105

Dodecahedron
★★★★
page 110

Symbols

Lines

– – – – – – – – – –   Valley fold, fold in front.

–·–·–·–·–·–   Mountain fold, fold behind.

—————————   Crease line.

· · · · · · · · · · · · · · · · · ·   X-ray or guide line.

Arrows

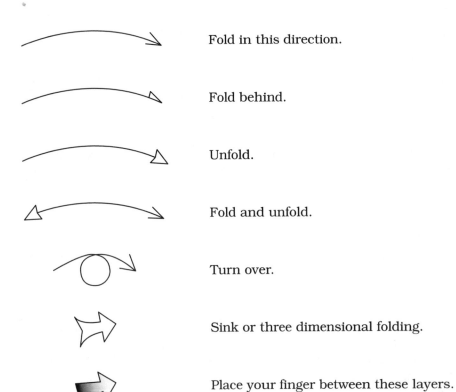

Fold in this direction.

Fold behind.

Unfold.

Fold and unfold.

Turn over.

Sink or three dimensional folding.

Place your finger between these layers.

Basic Folds

Squash Fold. In a squash fold, some paper is opened and then made flat. The shaded arrow shows where to place your finger.

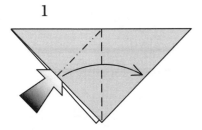

1

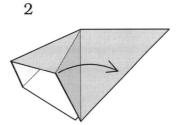

2

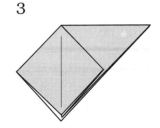

3

Squash-fold.

A three-dimensional intermediate step.

Inside Reverse Fold. In an inside reverse fold, some paper is folded between layers. Here are two examples.

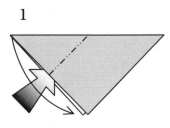

1

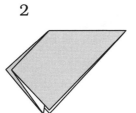

2

Reverse-fold.

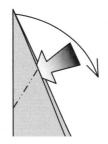

1

2

Reverse-fold.

Sink Fold. In a sink fold, some of the paper without edges is folded inside. To do this fold, much of the model must be unfolded.

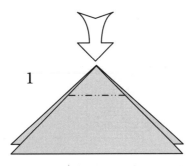

1

2

Sink.

Folding Polyhedra

Folding polyhedra from a single square sheet of paper so that they hold together requires different and new ways of folding. Because of this new adventure, I recommend you start with the simple or intermediate models shown below. Towards the back of the book information is given on the crease patterns or possible math used for some of the polyhedra.

Polyhedra require extensive use of three-dimensional folding. During that stage, be careful to understand how to interpret the valley and mountain fold lines. Where a mountain fold line typically means to fold behind, it could now refer to folding slightly behind. Another challenge during the three-dimensional folding is that the model might want to come apart and you wish for several extra hands.

Here are the typical stages in folding my polyhedra:

1. Stage 1 is finding the location of a landmark that is the key to folding the rest of the model. In some models this is found immediately and easily, while in others it could take over a page.

2. Stage 2 is in making all the prepatory creases. Often only small segments of a fold are creased. This is typically a couple of pages of simply folding and unfolding—the calm before the storm.

3. Then comes stage 3 where the main folding begins. The model becomes three-dimensional and the shape is realized.

4. Finally, stage 4 is the locking, tucking, inflating, or whatever it takes to close or finish the polyhedra. In some it is an easy tuck, but in others it takes some juggling to get all the loose ends to cooperate.

Some simple and intermediate models:

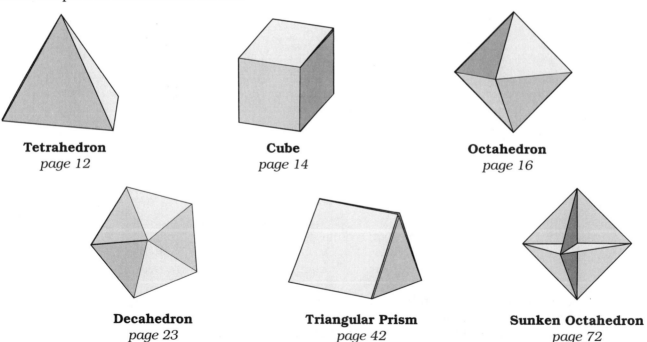

Tetrahedron
page 12

Cube
page 14

Octahedron
page 16

Decahedron
page 23

Triangular Prism
page 42

Sunken Octahedron
page 72

The Platonic Solids

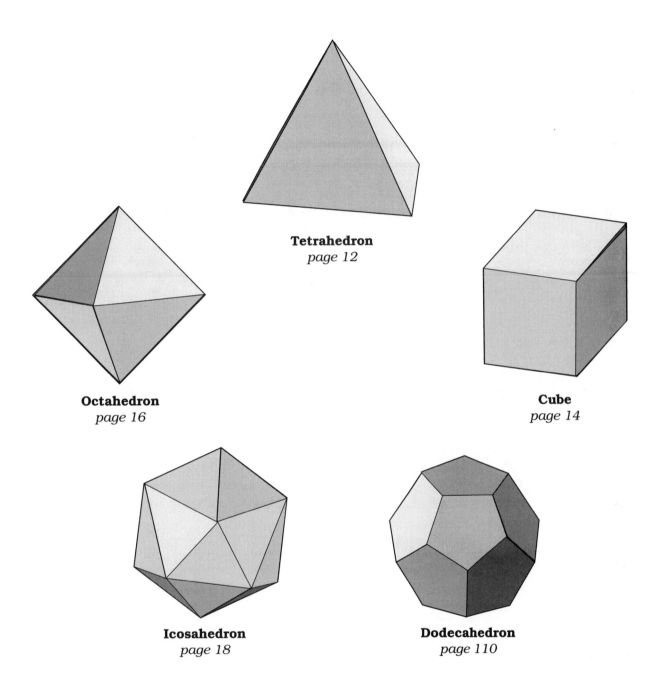

Tetrahedron
page 12

Octahedron
page 16

Cube
page 14

Icosahedron
page 18

Dodecahedron
page 110

The five regular solids, known as the Platonic solids, represent the first group of polyhedra. These are the only polyhedra with the following properties:
1. The faces of each are identical regular polygons.
2. The corners of each are alike.
3. Line segments connecting any two corners are on or inside the solid.

In folding these, the tetrahedron, cube, and octahedron are relatively easy, the icosahedron difficult, and the dodecahedron very difficult. Directions for the dodecahedron are shown towards the end of the book.

Tetrahedron

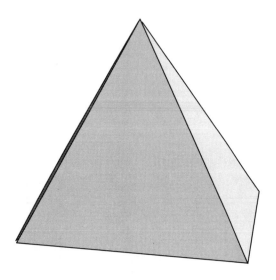

Composed of four equilateral triangles, this is the simplest of the five Platonic solids. Plato believed the tetrahedron represented fire because of its sharpness and simplicity. It is simple enough that the same folding pattern has been created independently by several origami artists. This is the perfect place to begin this journey.

1

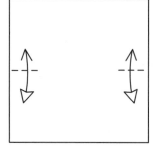

Fold and unfold on the left and right.

2

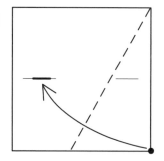

Bring the lower right corner to the center line.

3

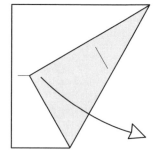

Unfold.

4

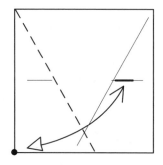

Fold and unfold.

5

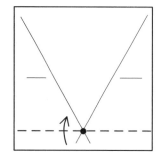

6

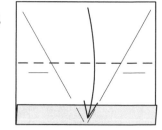

7

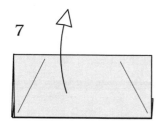

Unfold.

8

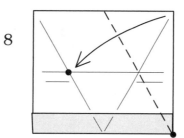

9

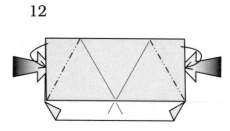

10

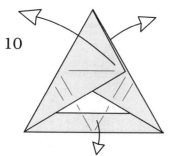

Unfold.

11

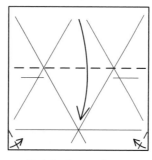

Fold along the
existing creases.

12

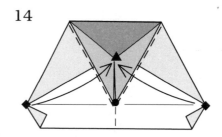

Reverse folds.

13

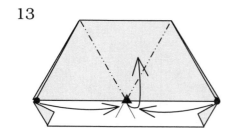

Lift up at the ▲ while the
dots meet. The model will
become three-dimensional.

14

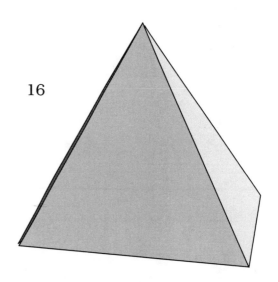

The ◆'s will meet
the ▲ at the top.

15

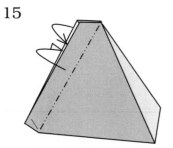

Tuck inside on
both sides.

16

Tetrahedron

Cube

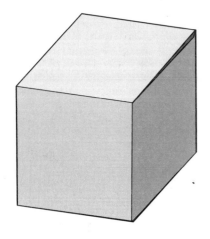

Designing a cube is an interesting problem. There already is a beautiful cube—the traditional waterbomb. The waterbomb wins hands down for its ease in folding, elegance, and the surprise at the end when you inflate a two-dimensional model. Instead, I chose to design a cube in which each side is a square panel with no crease on any side.

In keeping with the naming conventions of polyhedra, this could be called a hexahedron. Plato believed this regular polyhedron, composed of six squares, symbolized earth because of its stability.

1

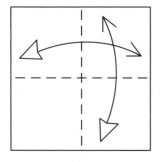

Fold and unfold.

2

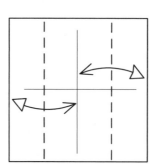

Fold and unfold.

3

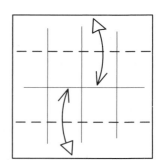

Fold and unfold.

4

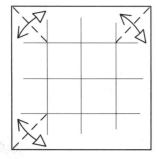

Fold and unfold.

5

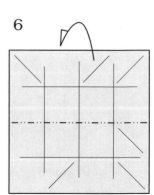

Fold and unfold.

6

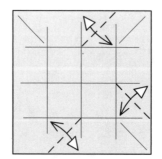

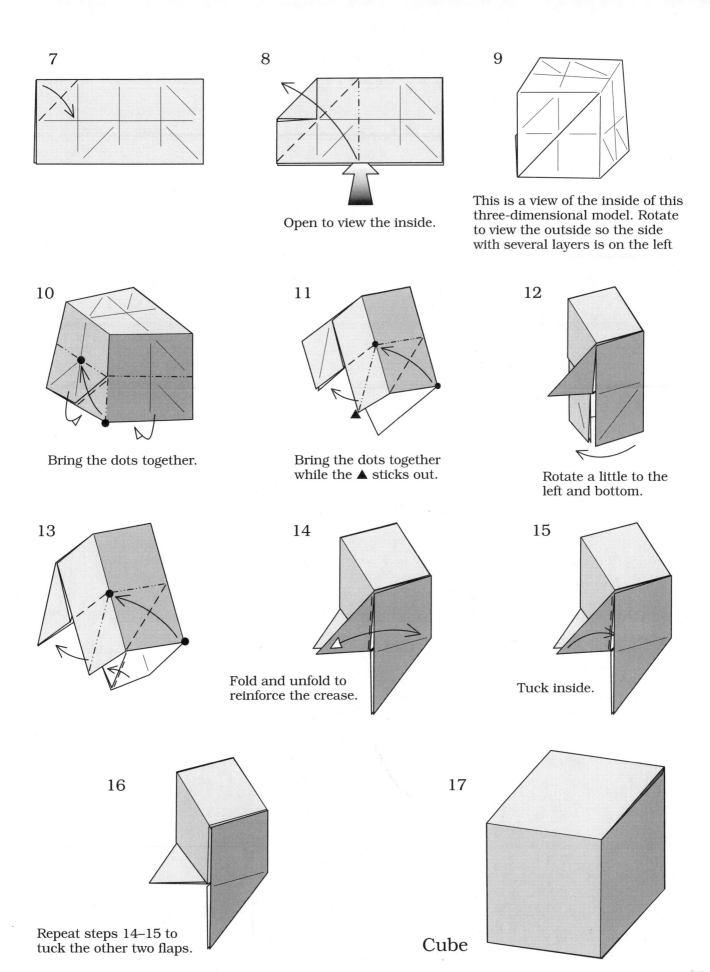

7

8

Open to view the inside.

9

This is a view of the inside of this three-dimensional model. Rotate to view the outside so the side with several layers is on the left

10

Bring the dots together.

11

Bring the dots together while the ▲ sticks out.

12

Rotate a little to the left and bottom.

13

14

Fold and unfold to reinforce the crease.

15

Tuck inside.

16

Repeat steps 14–15 to tuck the other two flaps.

17

Cube

Octahedron

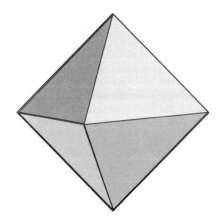

For this model, all the folding is two-dimensional until the last step when it is inflated.

This regular polyhedron, formed from eight equilateral triangles, represented air to Plato because it appears to be suspended. Like the other Platonic solids, the octahedron can be inscribed in a sphere where all the vertices meet the sphere. If the center of each side of the octahedron becomes the vertex (corner) of a new polyhedron, the new polyhedron would be a cube. Polyhedra related this way are called duals. So the dual of the octahedron is the cube. The dual of the tetrahedron is itself.

1

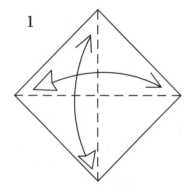

Fold and unfold along the diagonals. Rotate.

2

Fold and unfold to find the quarter mark.

3

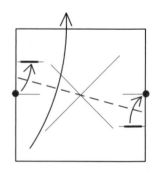

Align the dots and lines on the front and back.

4

Fold and unfold along the diagonals. Rotate.

5

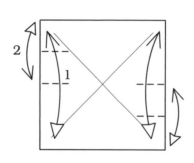

6

7

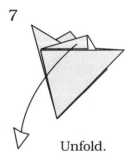

Unfold.

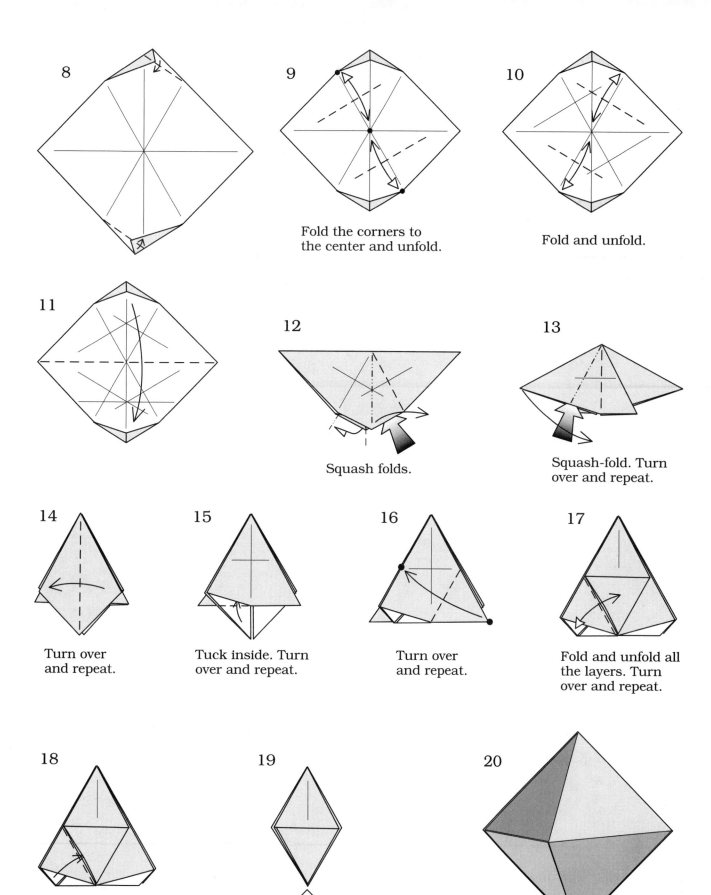

8

9

Fold the corners to
the center and unfold.

10

Fold and unfold.

11

12

Squash folds.

13

Squash-fold. Turn
over and repeat.

14

Turn over
and repeat.

15

Tuck inside. Turn
over and repeat.

16

Turn over
and repeat.

17

Fold and unfold all
the layers. Turn
over and repeat.

18

Tuck inside. Turn
over and repeat.

19

Inflate.

20

Octahedron

Icosahedron

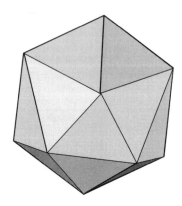

The icosahedron is a regular polyhedron composed of twenty equilateral triangles. Plato attributed this one to water because of its ability to roll. Its dual is the dodecahedron.

I thank Robert Lang for working out the folding method for finding the landmark in step 5.

1

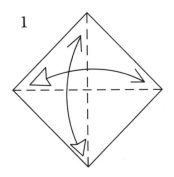

Fold and unfold.

2

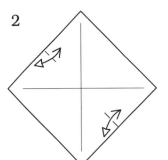

Fold and unfold, creasing at the ends.

3

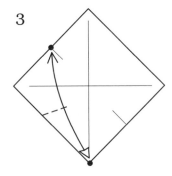

Fold and unfold bringing the dots together, creasing on the left.

4

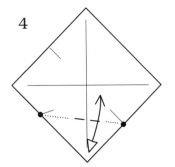

Fold and unfold, creasing on the diagonal.

5

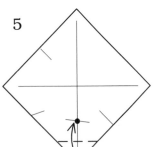

6

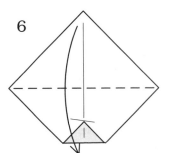

7

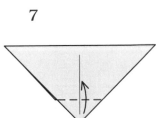

8

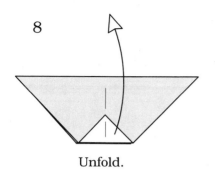

Unfold.

9

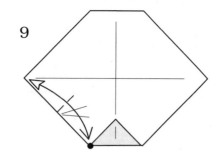

Fold and unfold.

10

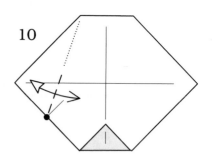

Fold and unfold.

11

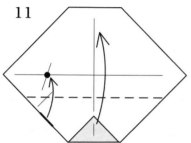

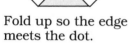

Fold up so the edge
meets the dot.

12

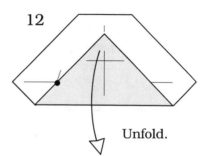

Unfold.

13

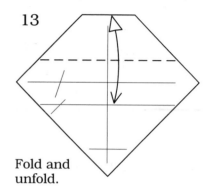

Fold and
unfold.

14

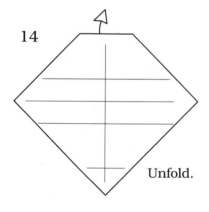

Unfold.

15

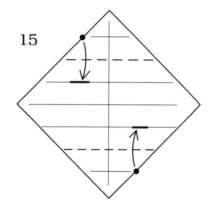

16

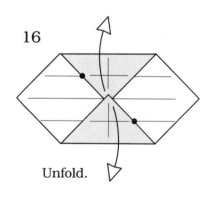

Unfold.

17

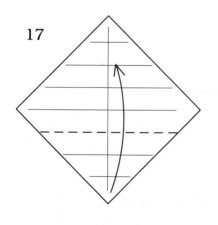

18

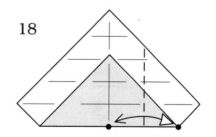

Fold and unfold.

19

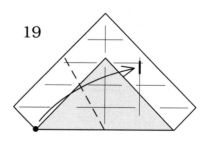

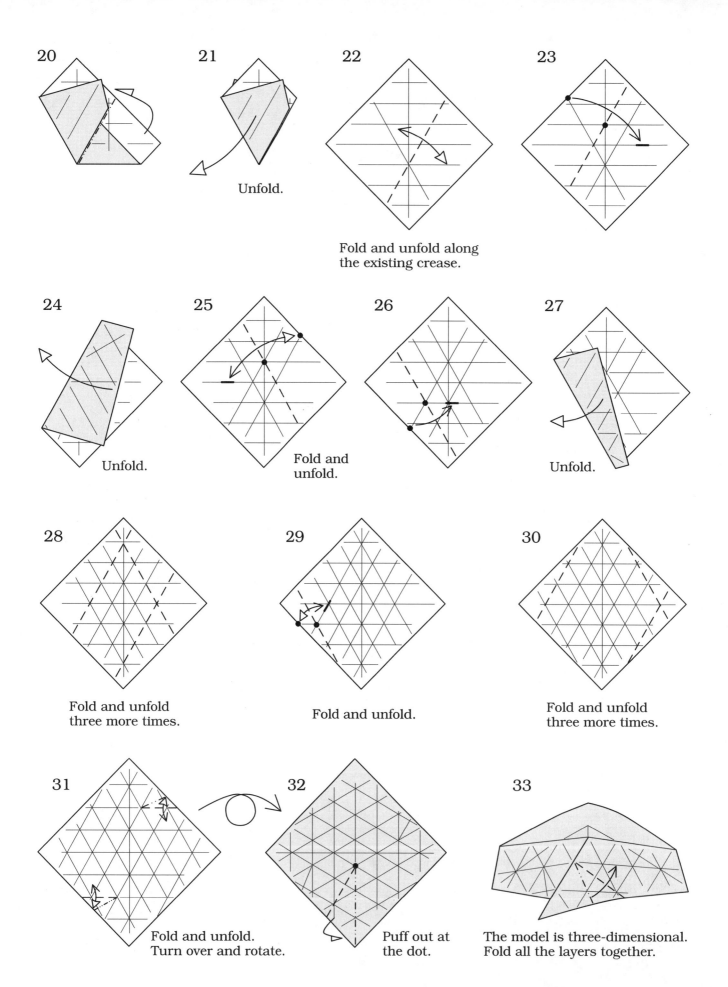

20

21

Unfold.

22

Fold and unfold along
the existing crease.

23

24

Unfold.

25

Fold and
unfold.

26

27

Unfold.

28

Fold and unfold
three more times.

29

Fold and unfold.

30

Fold and unfold
three more times.

31

Fold and unfold.
Turn over and rotate.

32

Puff out at
the dot.

33

The model is three-dimensional.
Fold all the layers together.

34

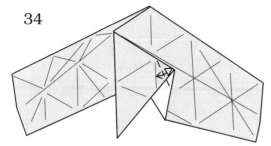

Fold and unfold.

35

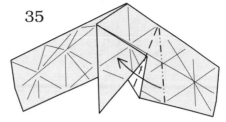

36

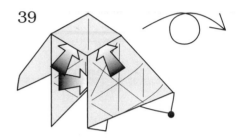

Unfold.

37

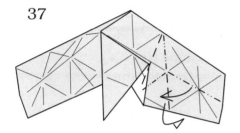

Keep the paper loose.

38

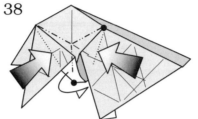

Tuck much of the paper inside so the lower dot meets the other one inside.

39

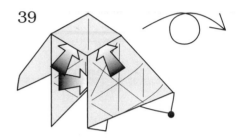

Note the orientation of the layers. Turn over so the dot goes to the front.

40

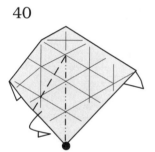

Repeat steps 32–39.

41

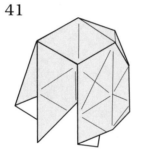

Rotate the top to the bottom.

42

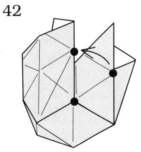

Puff out at the lower dot while bringing the other ones together.

43

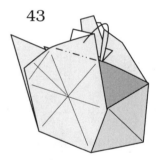

Wrap around the dark paper.

44

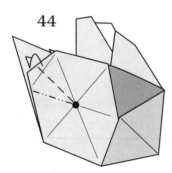

Puff out at the dot and tuck inside along existing creases. The mountain fold extends inside the model. Reach inside and press flaps flat against the inside of the model.

45

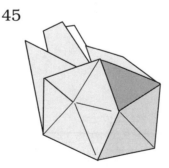

Turn over and repeat steps 42–44.

46

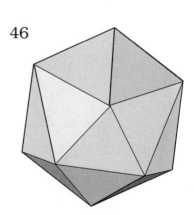

Icosahedron

Diamonds

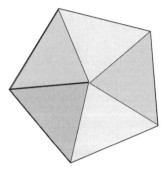

Decahedron
page 23

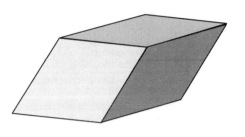

**Double Diamond
Hexahedron**
page 25

--- **Dipyramids** ---

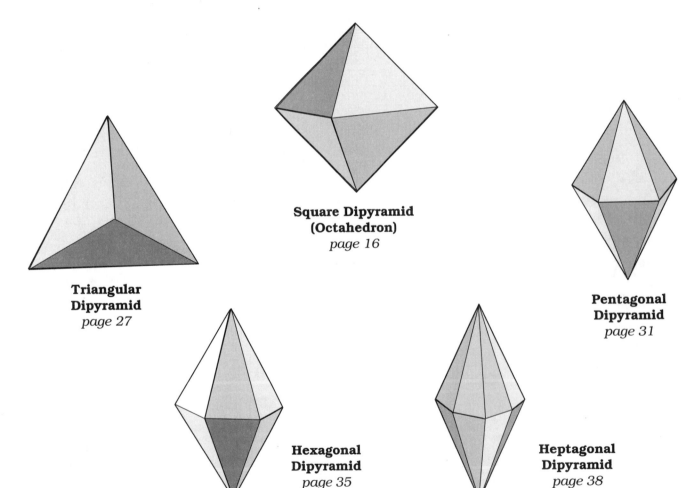

**Square Dipyramid
(Octahedron)**
page 16

**Triangular
Dipyramid**
page 27

**Pentagonal
Dipyramid**
page 31

**Hexagonal
Dipyramid**
page 35

**Heptagonal
Dipyramid**
page 38

Except for the double diamond hexahedron, these diamonds are
made of two pyramids connected at the base. The collection of
dipyramids are the duals of regular prisms with square sides.
Information on their angles is given on page 119.

Decahedron

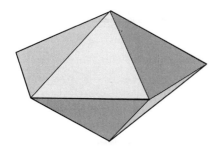

The decahedron is a general term for a ten-sided polyhedron. This one can also be called a pentagonal dipyramid. It is composed of equilateral triangles, resembling a space ship.

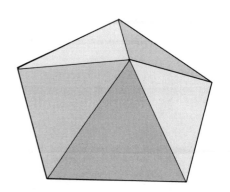

1

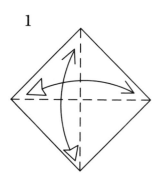

Fold and unfold along the diagonals.

2

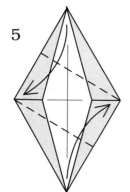

Fold and unfold.

3

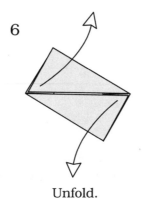

4

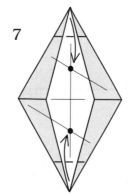

5

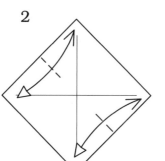

6

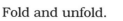

Unfold.

7

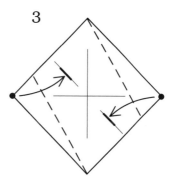

8

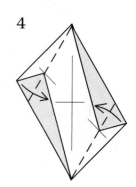

Fold and unfold.

9

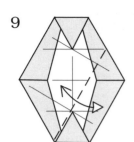

Fold and unfold.

10

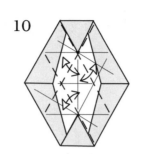

Fold and unfold
three more times.

11

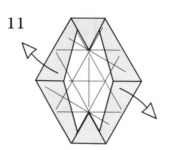

Unfold.

12

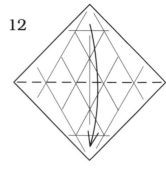

13

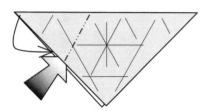

Reverse-fold.

14

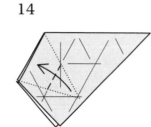

Fold both layers together inside.
The tip will be folded back.

15

16

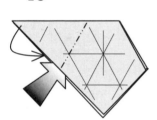

Repeat steps 13–14.

17

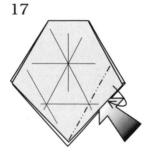

Reverse-fold on
the right. Turn
over and repeat.

18

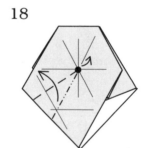

Lift up at the dot. Place
your finger inside to make
the top three-dimensional.
Turn over and repeat.

19

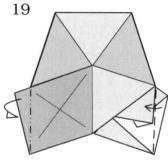

20

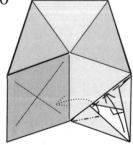

Tuck inside with
a squash fold.

21

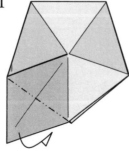

Tuck inside. Do not
make a squash fold.

22

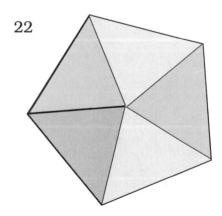

Decahedron

Double Diamond Hexahedron

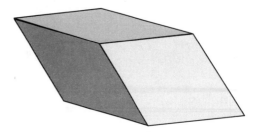

This polyhedron is made up of six
diamonds. Each diamond is
composed of two equilateral triangles.

Begin with step 12 of the Decahedron (page 23).

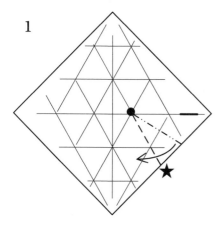

1

Push in at the dot as the model
becomes three-dimensional.
The ★ and bold line will meet
with the bold line on top.

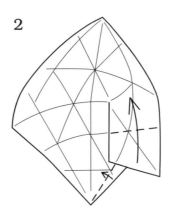

2

Squash-fold.

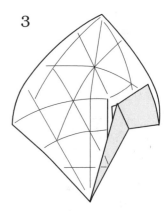

3

Rotate 180°.

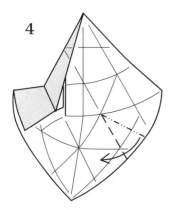

4

Repeat steps 1–2.

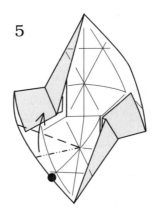

5

Valley-fold along the existing
crease so the dot will meet
the line with the valley fold.

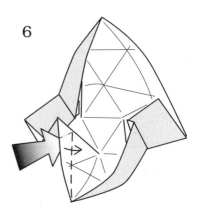

6

Squash-fold.

7

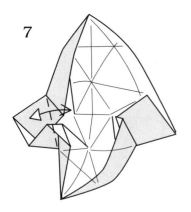

Fold and unfold.

8

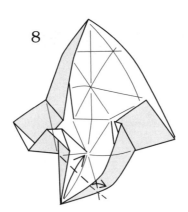

Squash-fold.

9

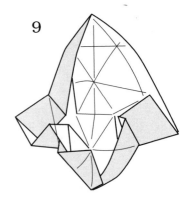

Rotate 180° and
repeat steps 5–8.

10

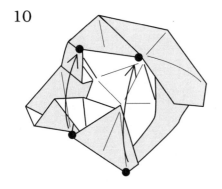

Bring the pairs
of dots together.

11

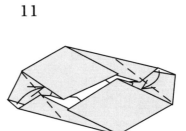

Tuck inside.

12

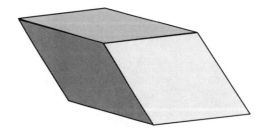

Double Diamond Hexahedron

Triangular Dipyramid

It is difficult to express this beautiful six-sided diamond in a two-dimensional picture. Each side is an isoceles triangle with sides proportional to 1, 1, 1.5, and the large angle is about 97.2°. Though the folding is relatively easy, the preliminary work necessary to find the unusual angles takes a bit of folding. There is no three-dimensional folding until it pops into shape at the last step.

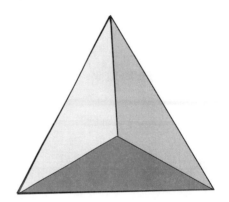

I thank Robert Lang for working out the folding method for finding the landmark in step 5.

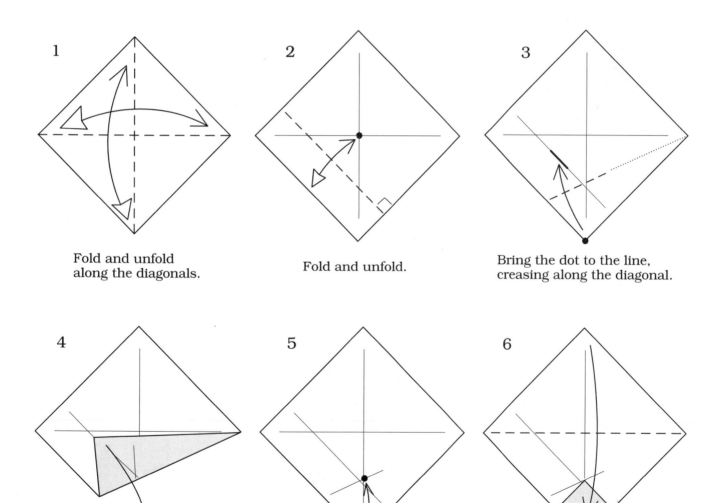

1 Fold and unfold along the diagonals.

2 Fold and unfold.

3 Bring the dot to the line, creasing along the diagonal.

4 Unfold.

5

6

7

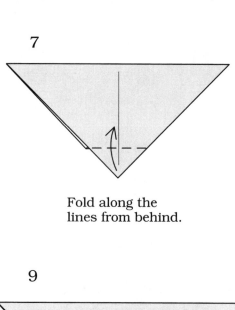

Fold along the
lines from behind.

8

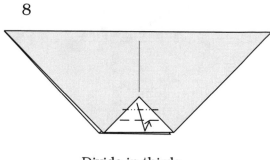

Divide in thirds.

9

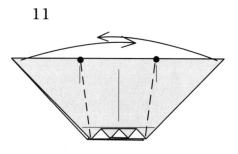

Fold inside and unfold.

10

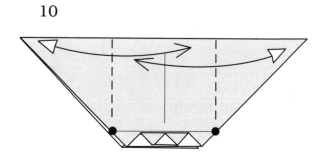

Fold and unfold.

11

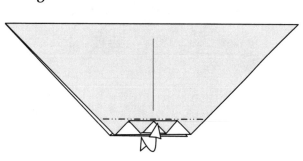

12

Unfold.

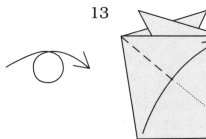

13

Only crease on the
upper half. A flap
will swing out.

14

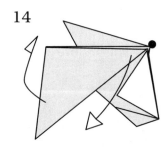

Hopefully the corners
at the dot meet or are
close. Unfold.

15

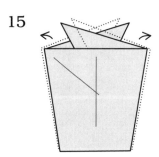

If the corners in step 14
were not close, adjust
the flaps a little.

16

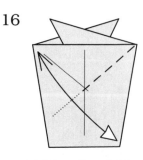

Fold and unfold.

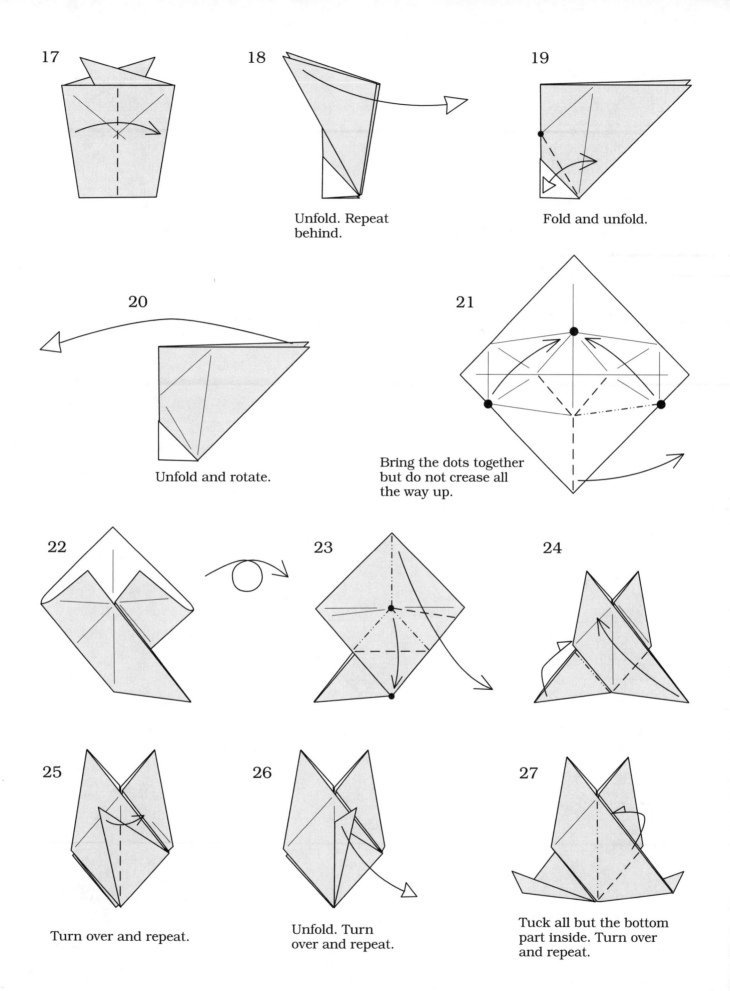

17

18

Unfold. Repeat
behind.

19

Fold and unfold.

20

Unfold and rotate.

21

Bring the dots together
but do not crease all
the way up.

22

23

24

25

Turn over and repeat.

26

Unfold. Turn
over and repeat.

27

Tuck all but the bottom
part inside. Turn over
and repeat.

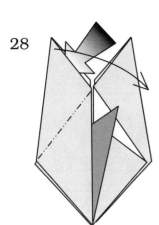

28

Fold behind the dark paper for this reverse-fold. Turn over and repeat.

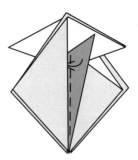

29

Tuck the dark paper inside. Turn over and repeat.

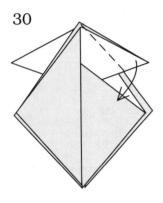

30

Turn over and repeat.

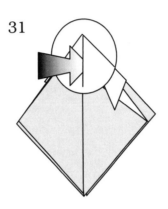

31

Note the pocket inside.

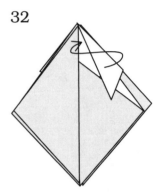

32

Tuck inside the pocket. Turn over and repeat.

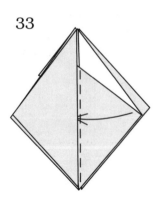

33

Tuck inside. Turn over and repeat.

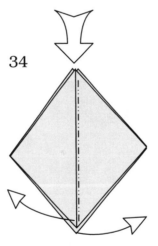

34

Pull apart or inflate to open.

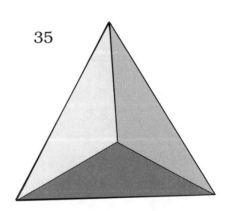

35

Triangular Dipyramid

Pentagonal Dipyramid

This is a ten-sided diamond composed of isoceles triangles. The small angle in each triangle is about 40°. The methods for folding this, the hexagonal and heptagonal dipyramids are similar.

The crease pattern in step 21 shows the location of the ten triangles on the square paper which will form the sides of this dipyramid. The task is to hide the paper not used for the sides. Of course this is the same method used in carving an elephant out of stone—simply carve away anything that does not look like an elephant.

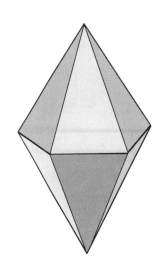

I thank Robert Lang for his method for finding the landmarks in the opening folds.

1

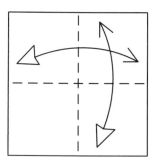

Fold and unfold.

2

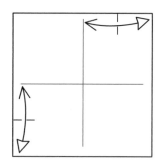

Fold and unfold.

3

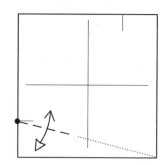

Fold and unfold, creasing on the left.

4

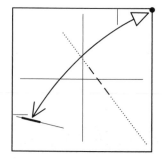

Fold and unfold, creasing on the horizontal lne.

5

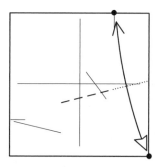

Fold and unfold, creasing on the vertical lne.

6

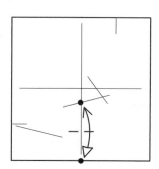

Fold and unfold, creasing on the vertical lne.

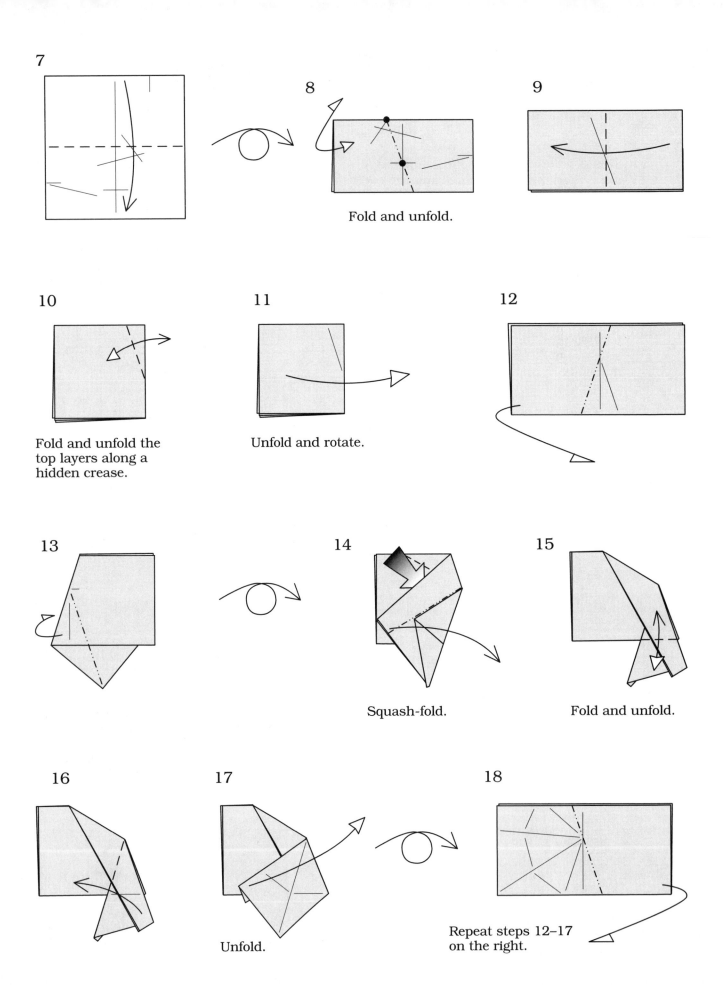

7

8

Fold and unfold.

9

10

Fold and unfold the
top layers along a
hidden crease.

11

Unfold and rotate.

12

13

14

Squash-fold.

15

Fold and unfold.

16

17

Unfold.

18

Repeat steps 12–17
on the right.

19

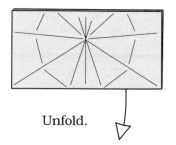

Unfold.

20

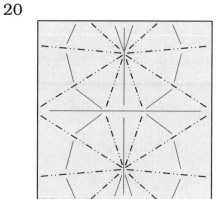

Make each of these a
mountain fold crease. Only
crease if they are not.

21

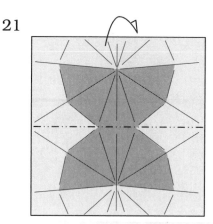

The dark regions will form
the sides of the dipyramid.

22

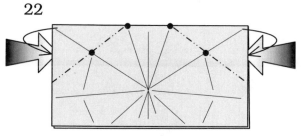

Reverse folds.

23

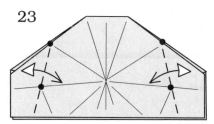

Fold and unfold.
Repeat behind.

24

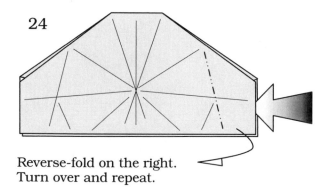

Reverse-fold on the right.
Turn over and repeat.

25

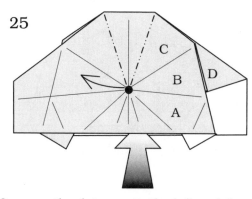

Open so the dot goes to the left and the
same spot on the back goes to the
right. The model will become
three-dimensional. Follow the triangles
A, B, C, and D in the next step.

26

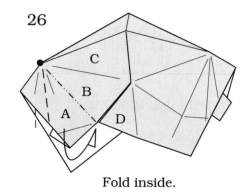

Fold inside.

27

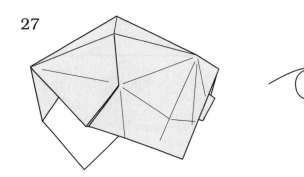

Pentagonal Dipyramid 33

28

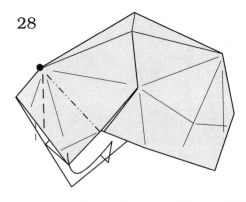

29

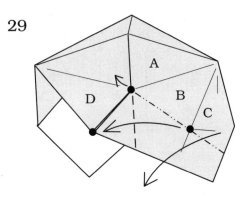

Lift up at the upper dot. Follow
the letters in the next step.

30

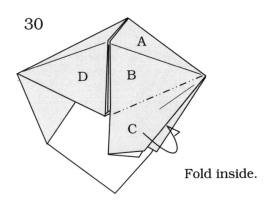

Fold inside.

31

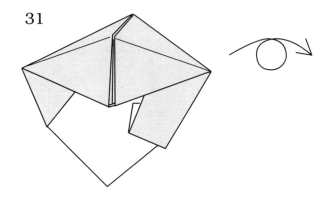

32

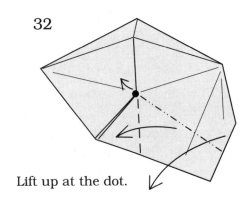

Lift up at the dot.

33

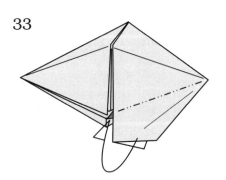

Note the pocket shown by the dark
paper (only a tiny part is visible).
Tuck into the pocket. Rotate.

34

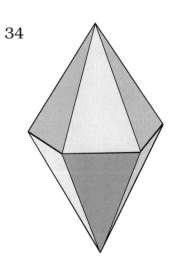

Pentagonal Dipyramid

Hexagonal Dipyramid

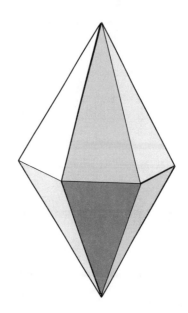

In this twelve-sided diamond, the angle at the top of the isoceles triangle about 29°.

1

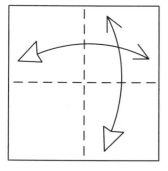

Fold and unfold.

2

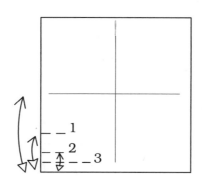

Divide in half three times. Make a longer crease for the last one.

3

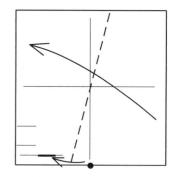

Bring the dot to the bold line while folding through the center.

4

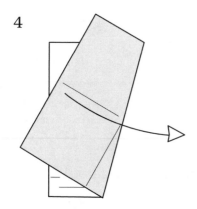

Unfold.

5

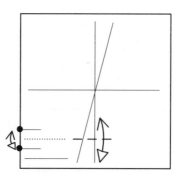

Fold half way between the creases by the center. Unfold.

6

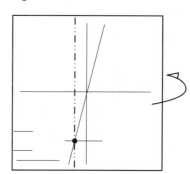

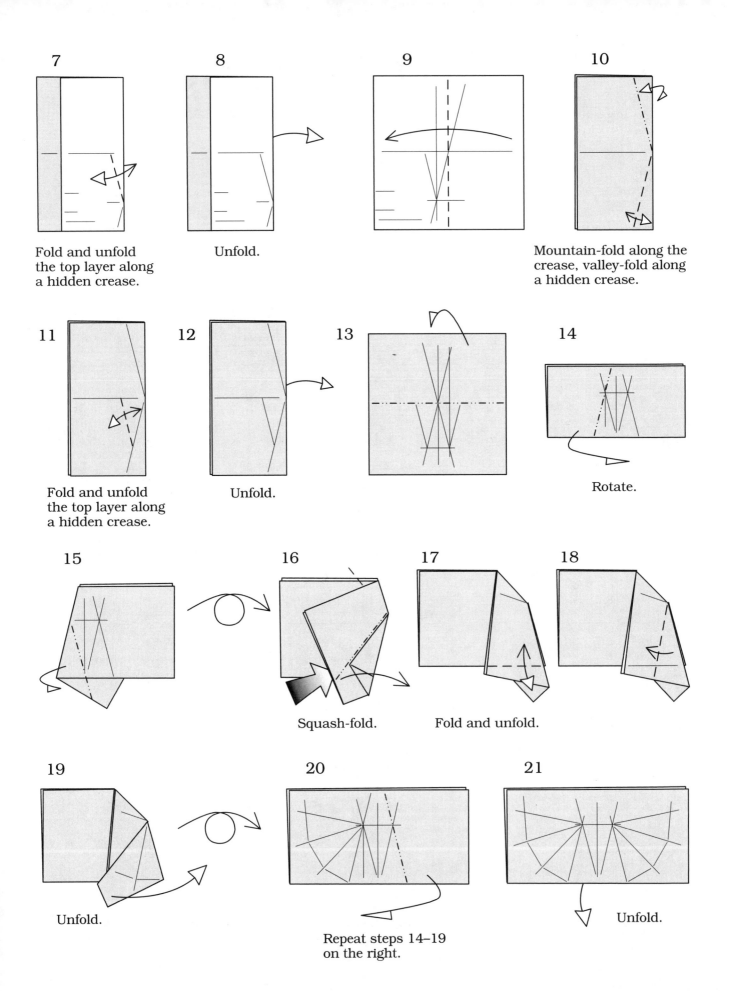

7

Fold and unfold
the top layer along
a hidden crease.

8

Unfold.

9

10

Mountain-fold along the
crease, valley-fold along
a hidden crease.

11

Fold and unfold
the top layer along
a hidden crease.

12

Unfold.

13

14

Rotate.

15

16

Squash-fold.

17

Fold and unfold.

18

19

Unfold.

20

Repeat steps 14–19
on the right.

21

Unfold.

22

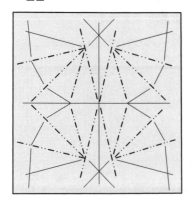

Make these mountain fold creases. Only crease if they are not.

23

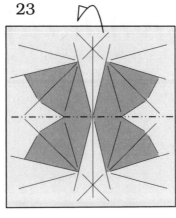

The dark regions will form the sides of the dipyramid.

24

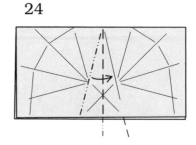

Turn over and repeat.

25

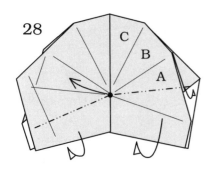

Note the direction of the layers by the large arrow. Make two reverse folds.

26

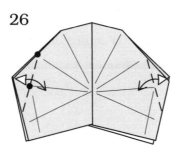

Fold and unfold. Repeat behind.

27

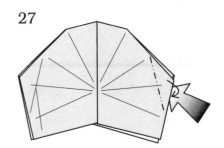

Reverse-fold on the right. Turn over and repeat.

28

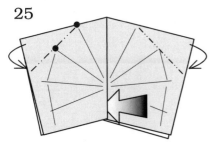

Bring the dot to the left while tucking inside. Turn over and repeat.

29

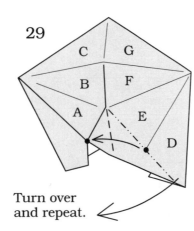

Turn over and repeat.

30

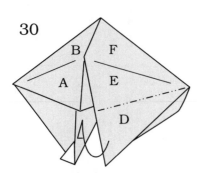

Tuck inside.

31

Tuck inside by wrapping around the flap to lock the diamond. Rotate.

32

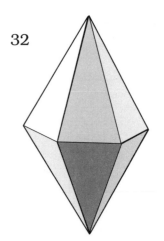

Hexagonal Dipyramid

Heptagonal Dipyramid

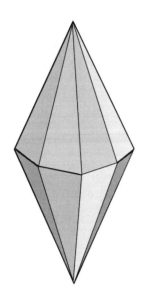

This is a fourteen-sided diamond composed of isoceles triangles. The small angle in each triangle is about 22°.

1

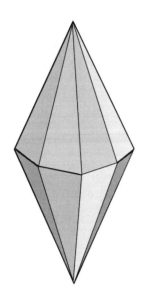

2

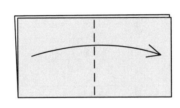

3

Unfold.

4

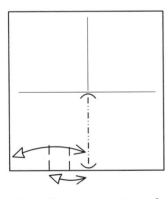

Note the orientation of the mountain fold crease. Fold and unfold.

5

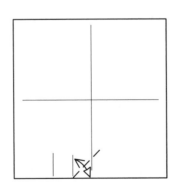

Fold and unfold.

6

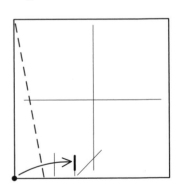

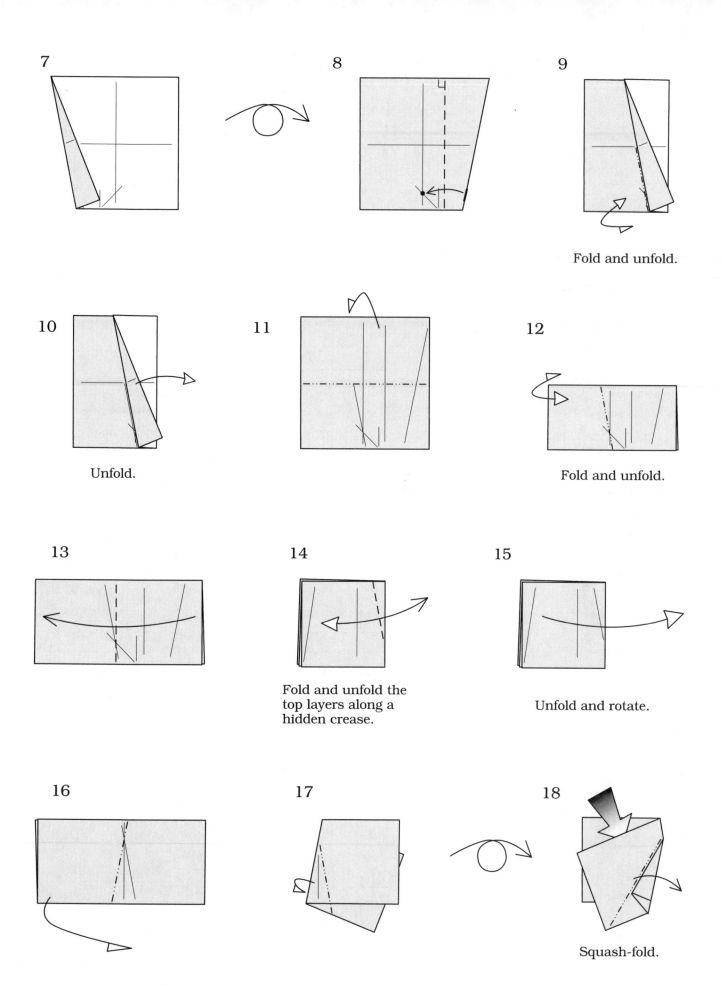

7

8

9

Fold and unfold.

10

Unfold.

11

12

Fold and unfold.

13

14

Fold and unfold the
top layers along a
hidden crease.

15

Unfold and rotate.

16

17

18

Squash-fold.

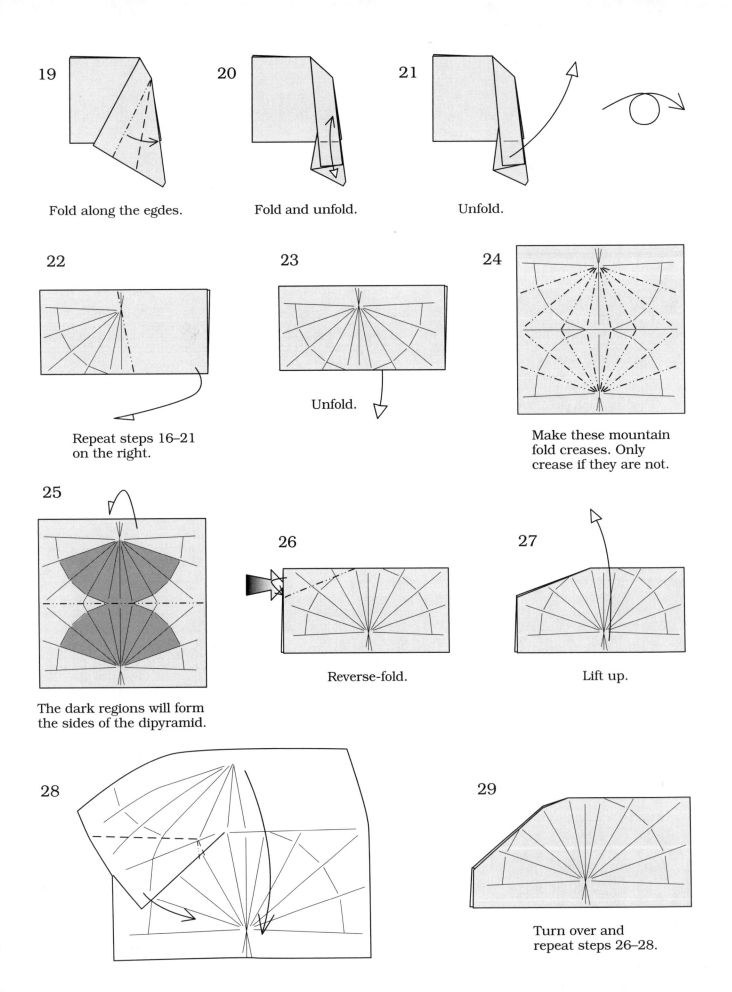

19 Fold along the egdes.

20 Fold and unfold.

21 Unfold.

22 Repeat steps 16–21 on the right.

23 Unfold.

24 Make these mountain fold creases. Only crease if they are not.

25 The dark regions will form the sides of the dipyramid.

26 Reverse-fold.

27 Lift up.

28

29 Turn over and repeat steps 26–28.

30

Fold and unfold.
Repeat behind.

31

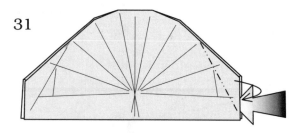

Reverse-fold on the right.
Turn over and repeat.

32

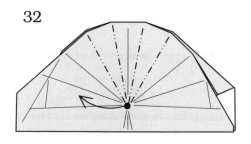

Open so the dot goes to the left
and the same spot on the back
goes to the right. The model
will become three-dimensional.

33

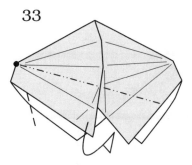

Turn over and repeat.

34

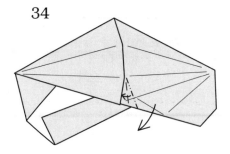

Turn over and repeat.

35

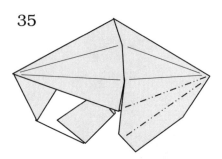

Mountain fold to reinforce the
creases. Turn over and repeat.

36

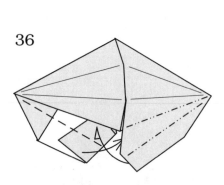

Tuck and interlock
the tabs. Rotate.

37

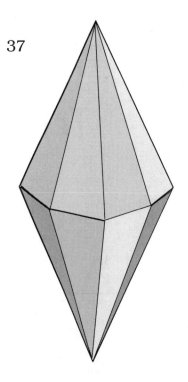

Heptagonal Dipyramid

Prisms

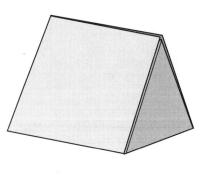

Triangular Prism
page 42

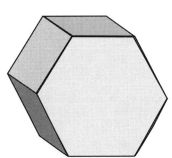

**Square Prism
(Cube)**
page 14

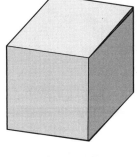

Pentagonal Prism
page 45

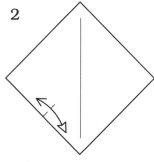

Hexagonal Prism
page 49

Prisms have rectangular sides connecting a pair of
identical polygons. This is a collection of prisms
with regular polygons and square sides. Their duals
are the dipyramids shown in the diamond section.

Triangular Prism

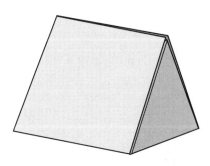

In 1665, Isaac Newton discovered
that white sunlight was made of
the colors of the rainbow by using
a triangular prism.

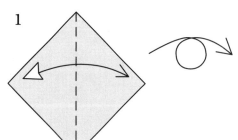

1

Fold and unfold.

2

Fold in half and unfold
creasing only on the edge.

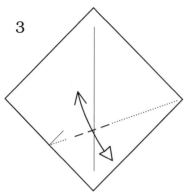

3

Fold and unfold creasing only on the diagonal.

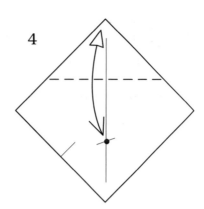

4

Fold and unfold. This divides the paper in thirds.

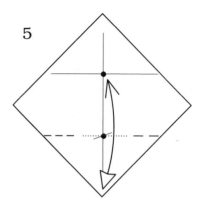

5

Fold and unfold creasing only at the ends.

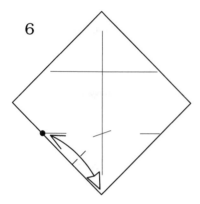

6

Fold in half and unfold creasing only on the edge.

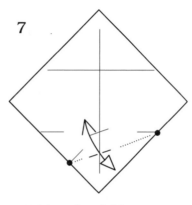

7

Fold and unfold creasing only on the diagonal.

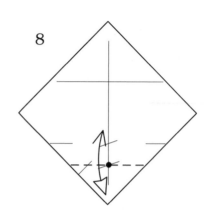

8

Fold and unfold.

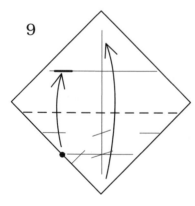

9

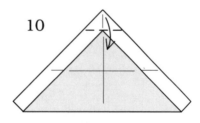

10

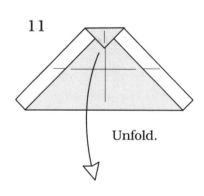

11

Unfold.

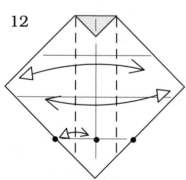

12

Fold and unfold.

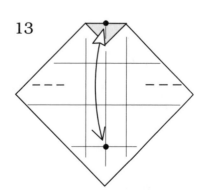

13

Fold and unfold creasing only at the ends.

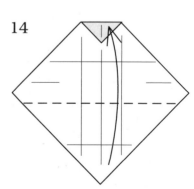

14

15

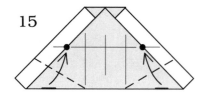

16

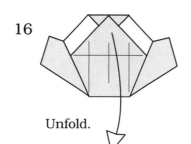

Unfold.

17

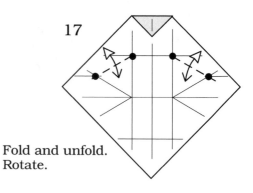

Fold and unfold.
Rotate.

18

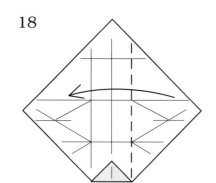

19

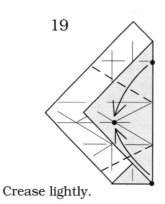

Crease lightly.

20

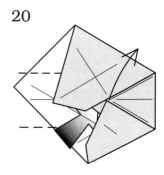

Lift up as the model
becomes three-dimensional.

21

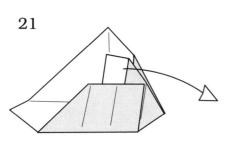

The model is
three-dimensional.
Unfold.

22

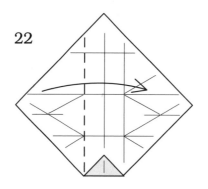

Repeat steps 18–21
on the left.

23

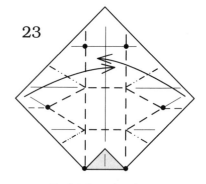

Refold on both
sides, interlocking
the layers.

24

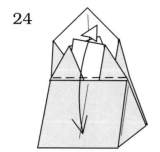

Fold and unfold.

25

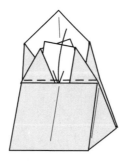

Tuck inside.

26

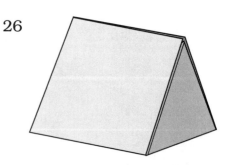

Triangular Prism

Pentagonal Prism

This pentagonal prism has five squares joining opposite pentagons. This and the other prisms are formed by folding a band of squares down the diagonal, and a pair of polygons (pentagons for this one) on opposite sides.

Many cameras use a pentagonal prism.

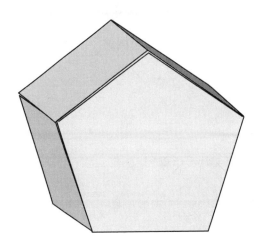

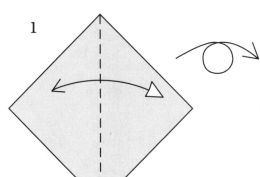

Fold and unfold.

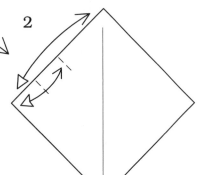

Fold and unfold to find the quarter mark.

Fold and unfold creasing on the diagonal.

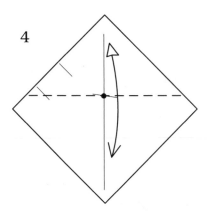

Fold and unfold. This divides the diagonal into 3/7 and 4/7.

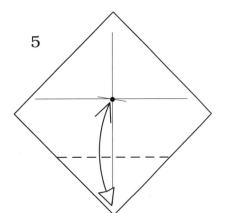

Fold and unfold.

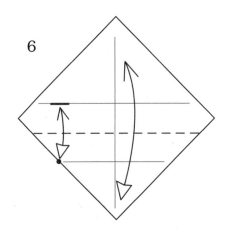

Fold and unfold.

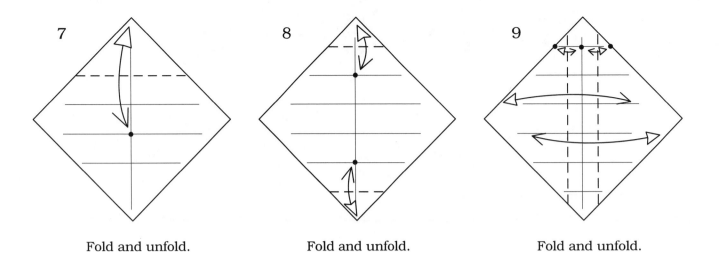

7 Fold and unfold.

8 Fold and unfold.

9 Fold and unfold.

10 Fold and unfold at the center.

11 Fold to the center creasing only at the ends. Unfold.

12 Fold and unfold.

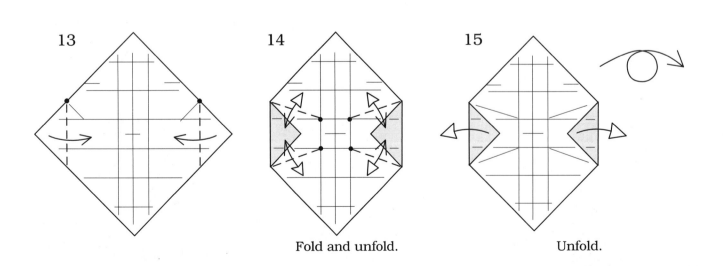

13

14 Fold and unfold.

15 Unfold.

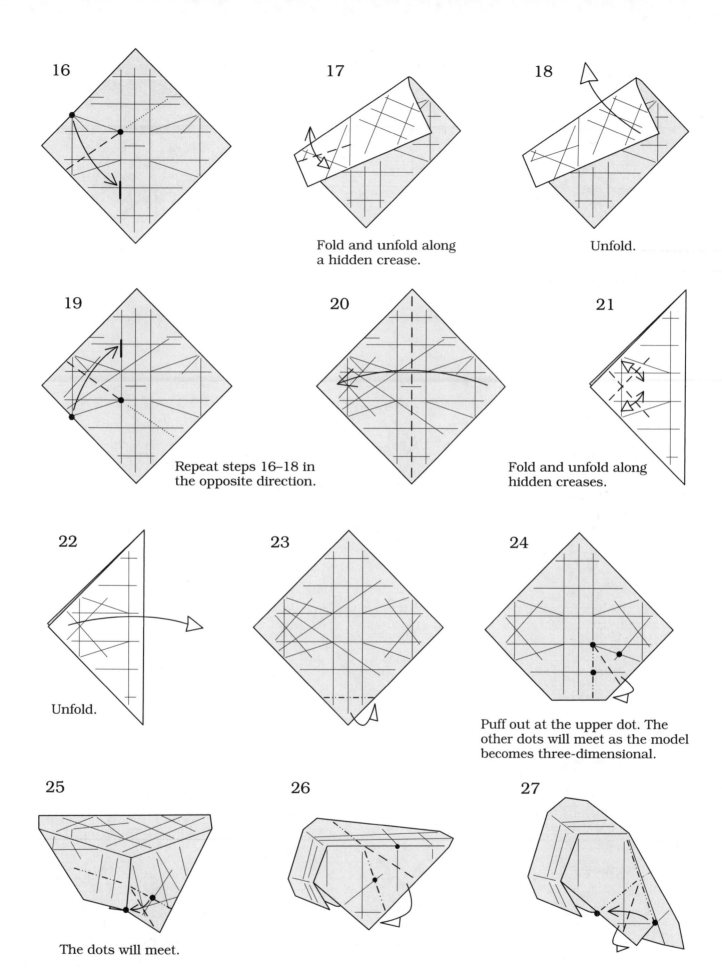

16

17

Fold and unfold along
a hidden crease.

18

Unfold.

19

Repeat steps 16–18 in
the opposite direction.

20

21

Fold and unfold along
hidden creases.

22

Unfold.

23

24

Puff out at the upper dot. The
other dots will meet as the model
becomes three-dimensional.

25

The dots will meet.

26

27

28

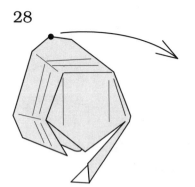

Rotate the back
corner to the right.

29

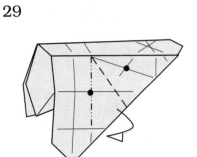

30

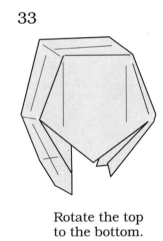

31

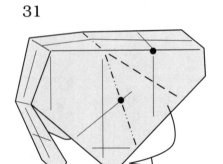

32

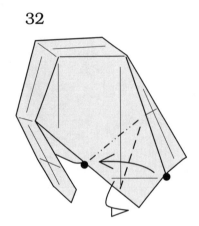

33

Rotate the top
to the bottom.

34

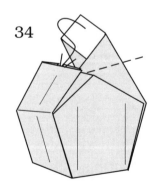

Tuck inside.

35

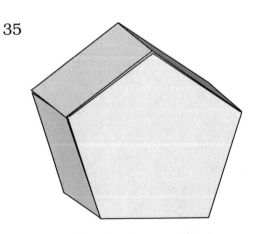

Pentagonal Prism

Hexagonal Prism

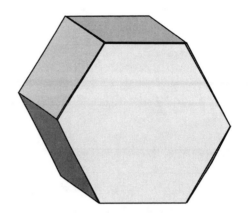

This prism has two hexagons at opposite faces and six squares going around.

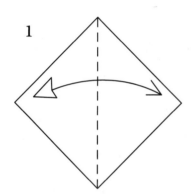

1

Fold and unfold.

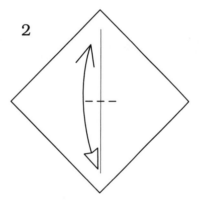

2

Fold and unfold creasing only at the center.

3

Fold and unfold creasing in the center.

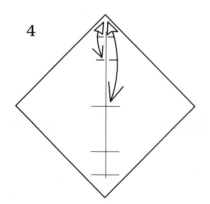

4

Fold and unfold creasing in the center.

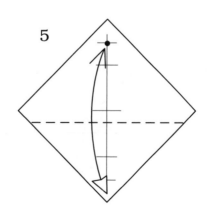

5

Fold and unfold.

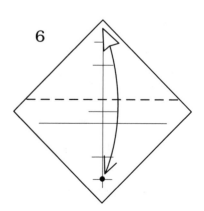

6

Fold and unfold.

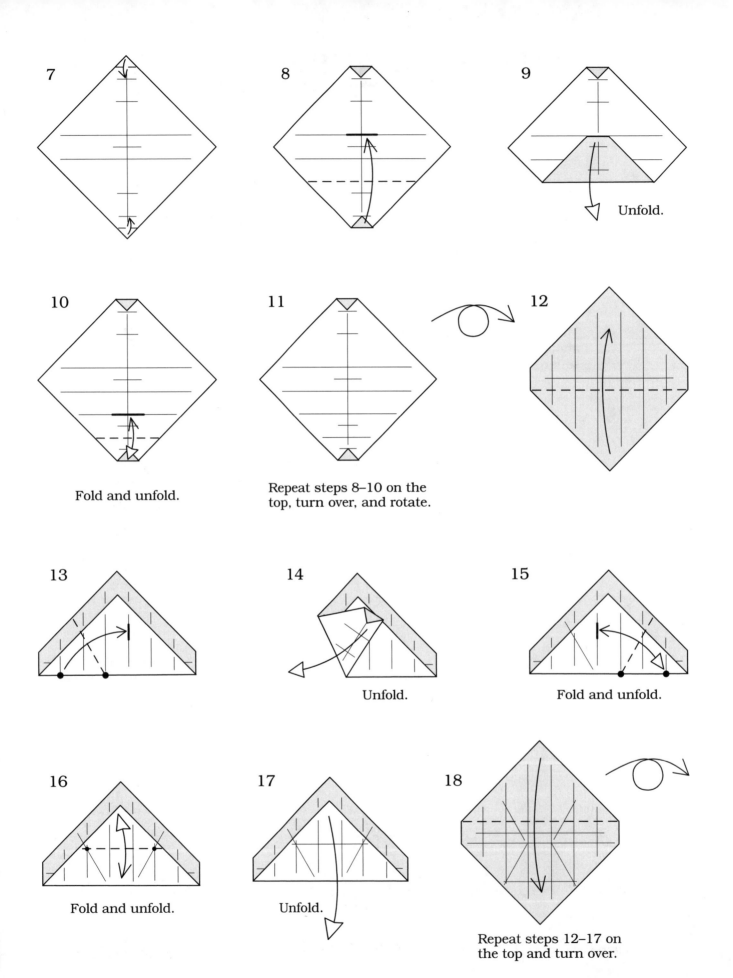

7

8

9

Unfold.

10

Fold and unfold.

11

Repeat steps 8–10 on the
top, turn over, and rotate.

12

13

14

Unfold.

15

Fold and unfold.

16

Fold and unfold.

17

Unfold.

18

Repeat steps 12–17 on
the top and turn over.

19

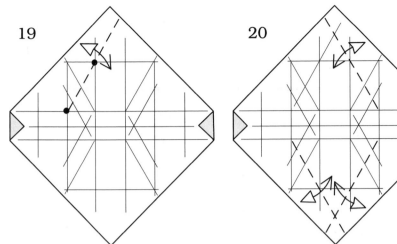

Fold and unfold.

20

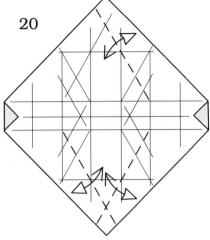

Fold and unfold.

21

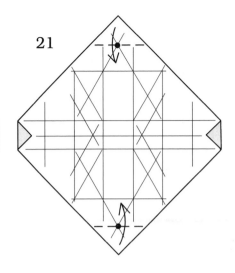

22

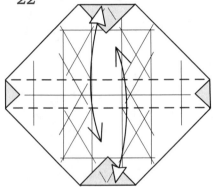

Fold and unfold.
Rotate.

23

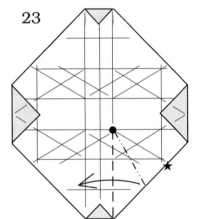

Fold the ★ to the valley-fold line. Push in at the dot.

24

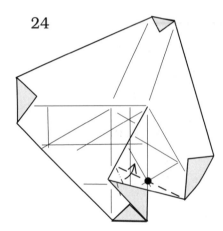

Squash-fold.

25

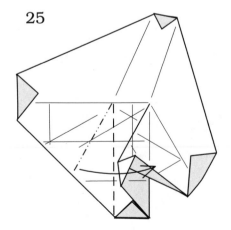

Repeat steps 23–24 on the left.

26

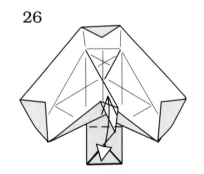

Fold and unfold.

27

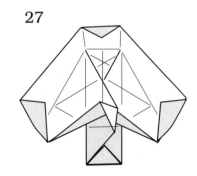

Repeat steps 23–26 on the top.

28

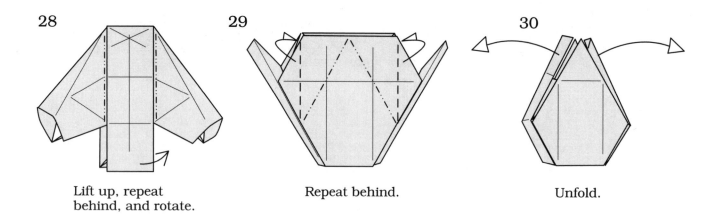

Lift up, repeat
behind, and rotate.

29

Repeat behind.

30

Unfold.

31

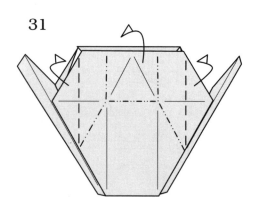

Form a rectangle at the top
going in. Repeat behind while
keeping the paper loose.

32

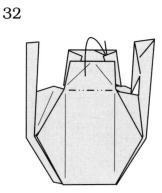

Tuck one of the top
sides inside the other.

33

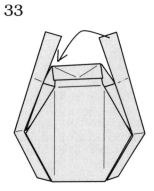

Cover the top.

34

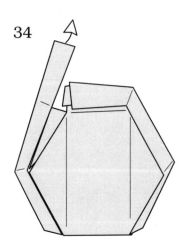

Unfold the tip.

35

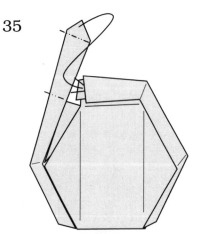

Tuck all the
way inside.

36

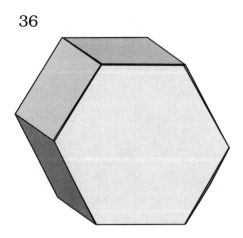

Hexagonal Prism

Based on the Octahedron

Six-Pointed Star
page 54

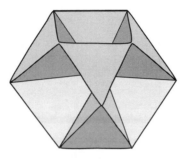

Octahemioctahedron
page 57

Dimpled Octahedron
page 67

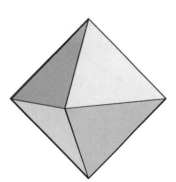

Octahedron
page 16

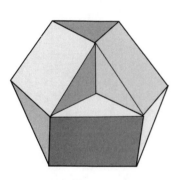

Cubehemioctahedron
page 60

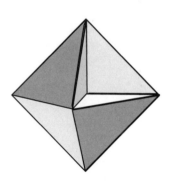

Heptahedron
page 63

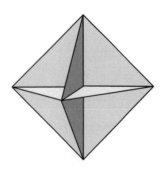

Sunken Octahedron
page 72

This collection of models are related by the octahedron. The six-pointed star comes from a collapsed form of the octahedron. The octahemioctahedron and dimpled octahedron have sunken corners. The cubehemioctahedron has its roots in the cube. Alternate sides of the heptahedron are indented. The sunken octahedron is shown in the next section.

Six-Pointed Star

Stars can be formed from collapsed polyhedra. (Is that deep or what?) This six-pointed star comes from the six vertices of an octahedron. It was designed as a collapsed octahedron though the octahedron is hidden in the folding procedure.

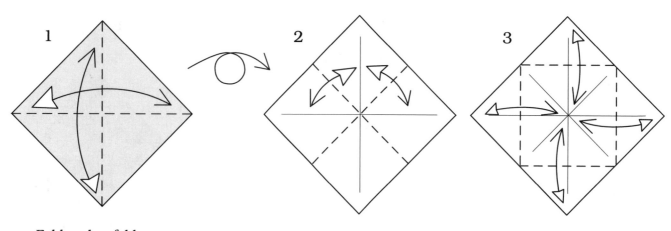

1

Fold and unfold along the diagonals.

2

Fold and unfold.

3

Fold and unfold.

4

Collapse the square by bringing the four corners together.

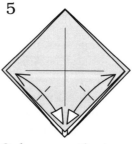

5

Only crease the top layer by the edges. Fold and unfold in half.

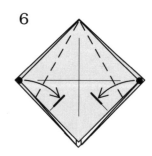

6

Repeat behind.

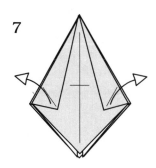

7

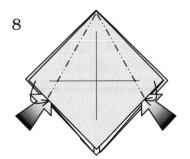

8

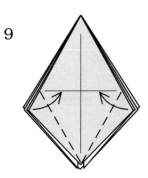

9

Unfold. Repeat behind.

Reverse folds.
Repeat behind.

Repeat behind.

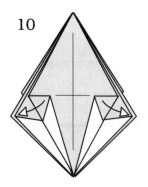

10

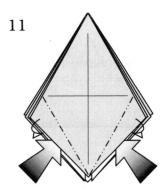

11

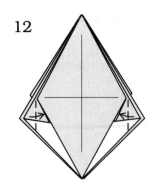

12

Unfold. Repeat
behind.

Reverse folds.
Repeat behind.

Repeat behind.

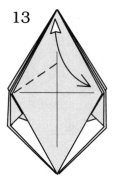

13

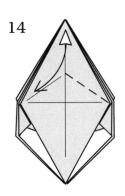

14

15

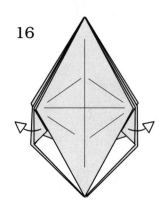

16

Fold all the layers
together and unfold.

Fold and unfold.

Fold and unfold.
Repeat behind.

Unfold. Repeat
behind.

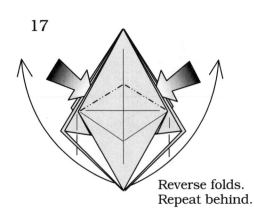

17

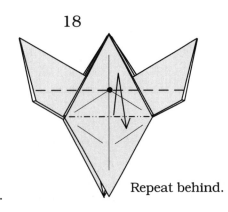

18

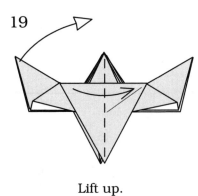

19

Reverse folds.
Repeat behind.

Repeat behind.

Lift up.

Six-Pointed Star 55

20

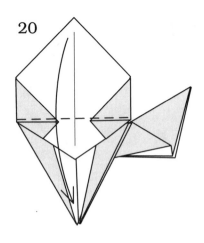

21

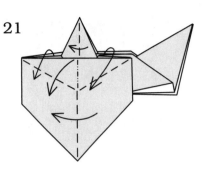

Fold down two flaps
on the left and right.

22

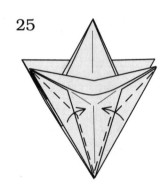

Repeat steps 19–21
on the right.

23

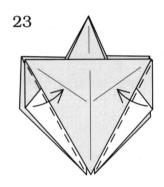

Repeat behind.

24

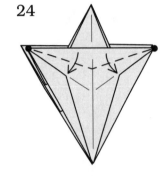

The corners with the dots will
come out as the model
becomes three-dimensional.

25

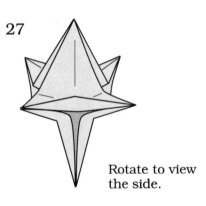

Fold towards the center.

26

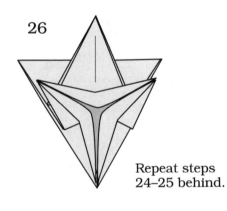

Repeat steps
24–25 behind.

27

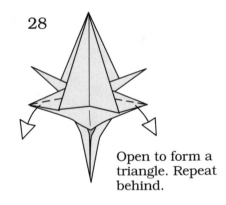

Rotate to view
the side.

28

Open to form a
triangle. Repeat
behind.

29

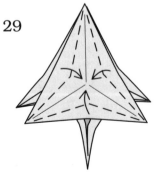

Fold towards the
center. Repeat behind.

30

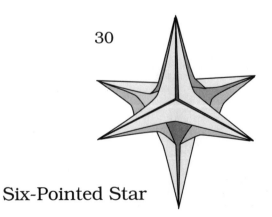

Six-Pointed Star

Octahemioctahedron

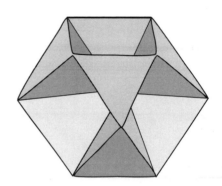

This comes from an octahedron with
sunken corners. A similar shape is the
cubehemioctahedron which comes from
a cube with sunken corners.

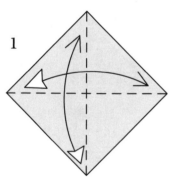

1

Fold and unfold
along the diagonals.

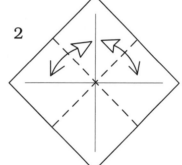

2

Fold and unfold.

3

Collapse the square
by bringing the four
corners together.

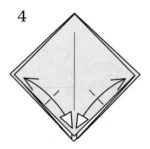

4

Only crease the top
layer by the edges. Fold
and unfold in half.

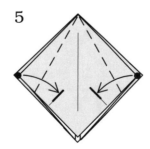

5

Repeat behind.

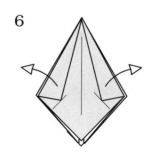

6

Unfold. Repeat behind.

7

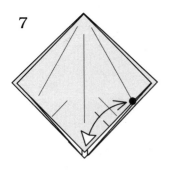

Fold and unfold creasing on the edge.

8

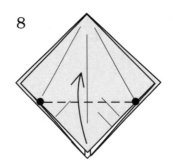

9

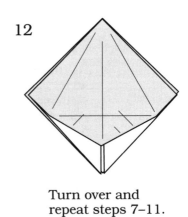

Fold the dot to the crease.

10

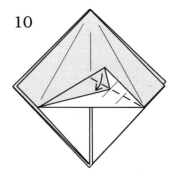

11

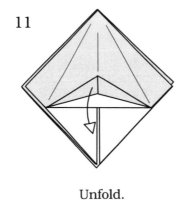

Unfold.

12

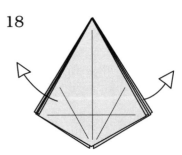

Turn over and repeat steps 7–11.

13

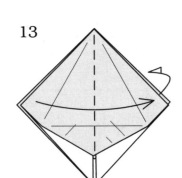

14

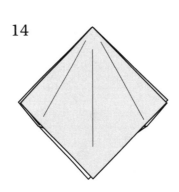

Repeat steps 7–11 on the front and back.

15

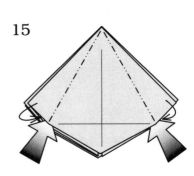

Reverse folds. Repeat behind.

16

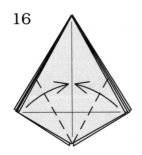

Fold a couple of layers together. Repeat behind.

17

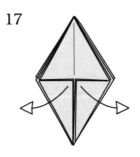

Unfold. Repeat behind.

18

Lift the top two layers on the left and the bottom two layers on the right.

19

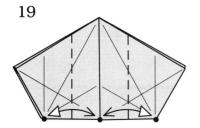

Fold and unfold
all the layers.

20

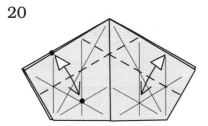

Fold and unfold
all the layers.

21

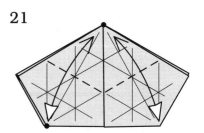

Fold and unfold
all the layers.

22

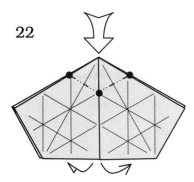

Sink at the top and open
at the bottom. Keep the
paper locked at the dots.

23

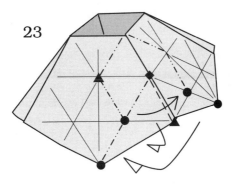

To form a sunken square:
1. Push in at the ◆.
2. Bring the pairs of dots together.
3. The ▲'s meet inside.
Much of the paper will be tucked
inside.

24

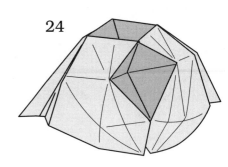

Repeat step 23 on
the three other sides.

25

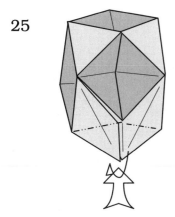

This sink is formed by four
connected reverse folds.

26

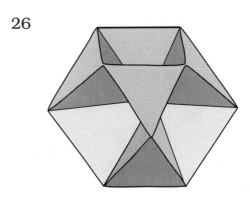

Octahemioctahedron

Cubehemioctahedron

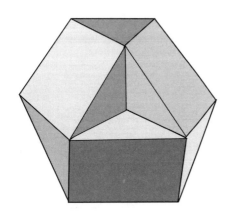

The cubehemioctahedron is basically a cube with sunken corners. However, trying to sink the corners of the cube shown earlier would be quite difficult.

1

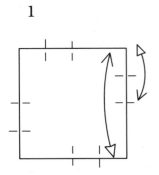

Make small marks by folding and unfolding in quarters.

2

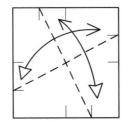

Fold and unfold.

3

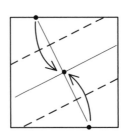

4

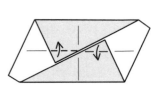

5

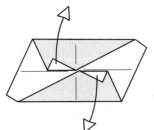

6

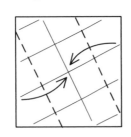

Repeat steps 3–5 in the opposite direction.

7

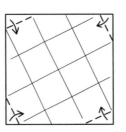

Fold along the creases.

8

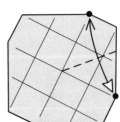

Fold and unfold.

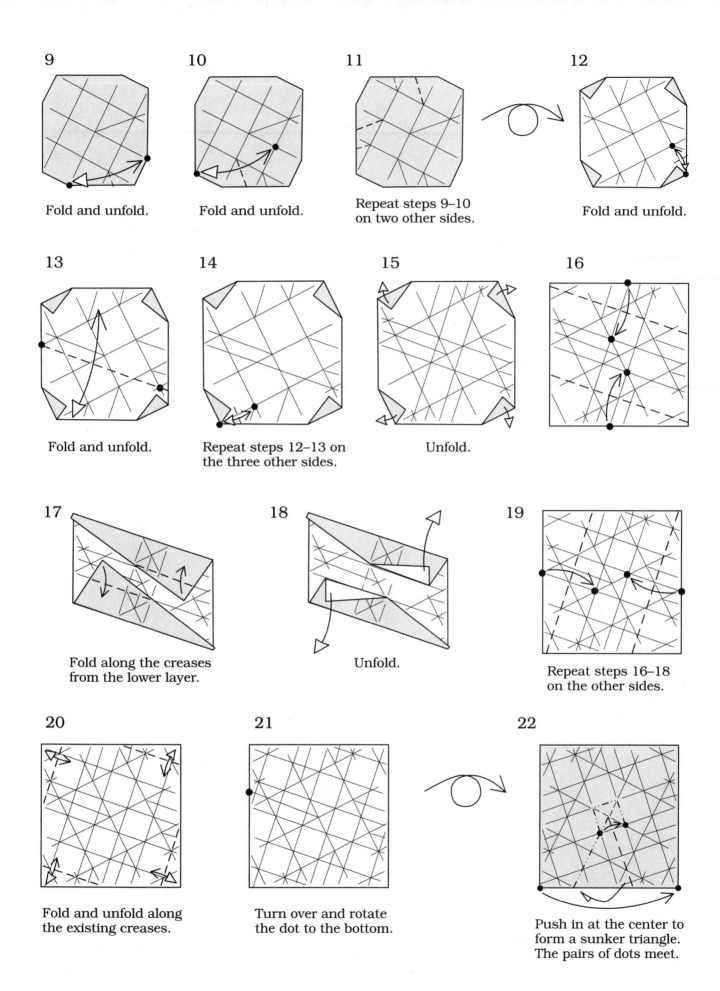

9

Fold and unfold.

10

Fold and unfold.

11

Repeat steps 9–10
on two other sides.

12

Fold and unfold.

13

Fold and unfold.

14

Repeat steps 12–13 on
the three other sides.

15

Unfold.

16

17

Fold along the creases
from the lower layer.

18

Unfold.

19

Repeat steps 16–18
on the other sides.

20

Fold and unfold along
the existing creases.

21

Turn over and rotate
the dot to the bottom.

22

Push in at the center to
form a sunker triangle.
The pairs of dots meet.

23

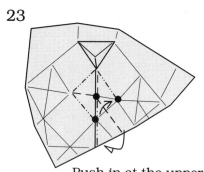

Push in at the upper dot
to form a sunken triangle.

24

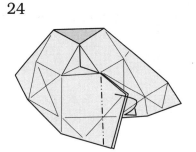

Fold both
layers together.

25

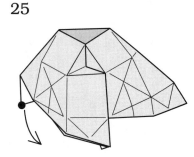

Rotate so the corner with the
dot shows at the front left.

26

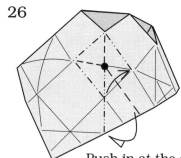

Push in at the dot to
form a sunken triangle.

27

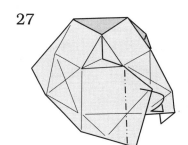

28

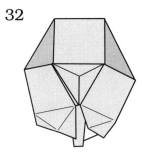

Repeat steps 26–27 on
the corner with the dot.

29

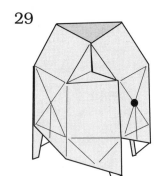

Rotate the dot
to the center.

30

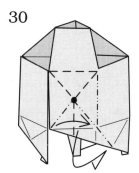

Push in at the dot to
form a sunken triangle.

31

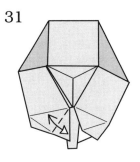

Fold and unfold.

32

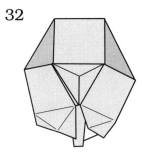

Repeat steps 30–31
two more times
going around.

33

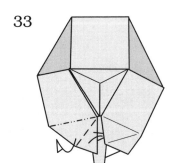

Begin to form the bottom sunken
triangle by folding toward the
inside center and tucking.

34

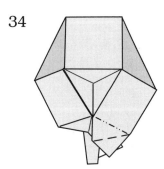

Repeat step 33 two more
times to complete the
bottom sunken triangle.

35

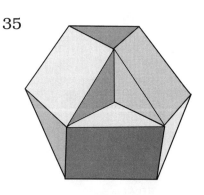

Cubehemioctahedron

Heptahedron

For this polyhedron, four sides are indented towards the center. It is named a heptahedron for its seven sides: four outer sides (same as the octahedron) and three center sides representing the x, y, and z axes. It can also called a tetrahemihexahedron. This interesting shape combines equilateral triangles with isoceles right triangles.

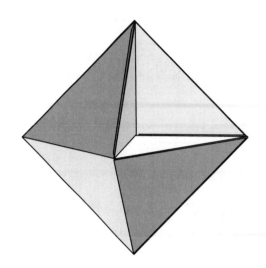

1

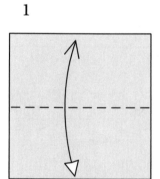

Fold and unfold.

2

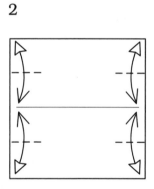

Fold and unfold to find the quarter marks.

3

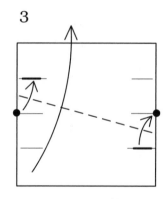

Align the dots and lines on the front and back.

4

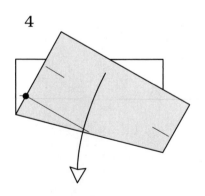

Unfold.

5

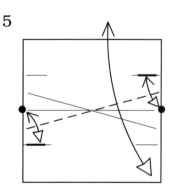

Fold and unfold.

6

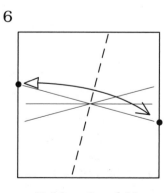

Fold and unfold.

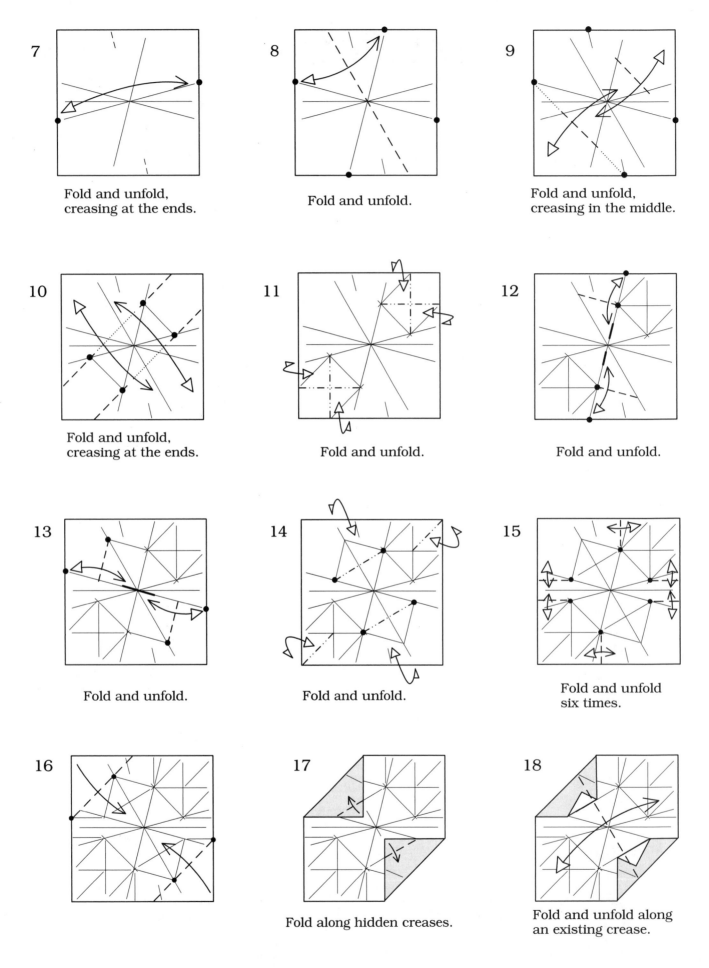

7 Fold and unfold, creasing at the ends.

8 Fold and unfold.

9 Fold and unfold, creasing in the middle.

10 Fold and unfold, creasing at the ends.

11 Fold and unfold.

12 Fold and unfold.

13 Fold and unfold.

14 Fold and unfold.

15 Fold and unfold six times.

16

17 Fold along hidden creases.

18 Fold and unfold along an existing crease.

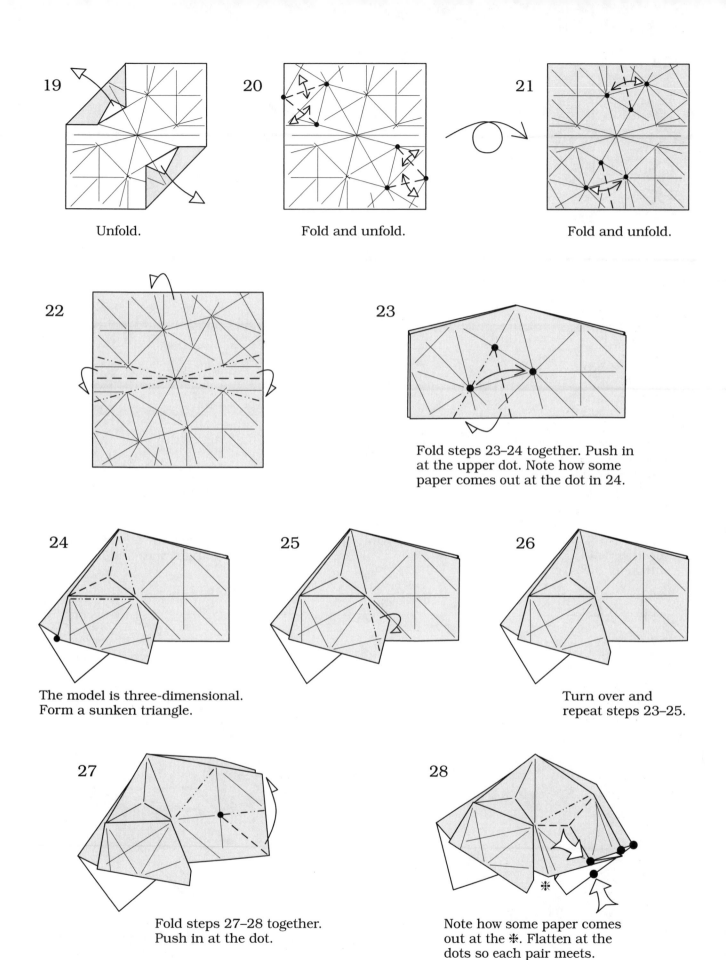

19 Unfold.

20 Fold and unfold.

21 Fold and unfold.

22

23 Fold steps 23–24 together. Push in at the upper dot. Note how some paper comes out at the dot in 24.

24 The model is three-dimensional. Form a sunken triangle.

25

26 Turn over and repeat steps 23–25.

27 Fold steps 27–28 together. Push in at the dot.

28 Note how some paper comes out at the ✳. Flatten at the dots so each pair meets.

Heptahedron 65

29

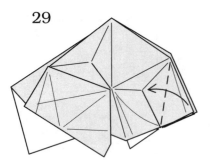

Fold all the
layers together.

30

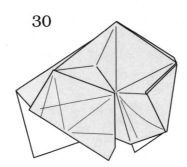

Turn over and
repeat steps 27–29.

31

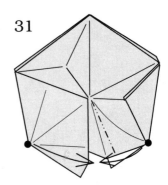

Bring the dots
together. Rotate.

32

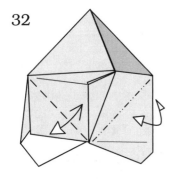

Flatten the flaps
together. Fold and
unfold all the layers.

33

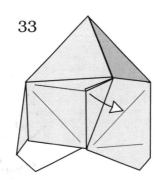

Unfold.

34

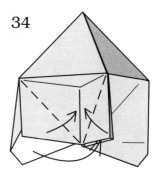

Tuck the left flap into the
right ones and flatten.

35

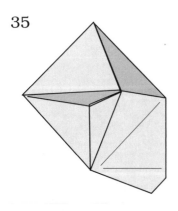

Turn over and
repeat step 34.

36

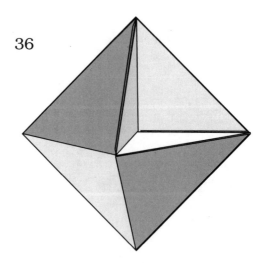

Heptahedron

Dimpled Octahedron

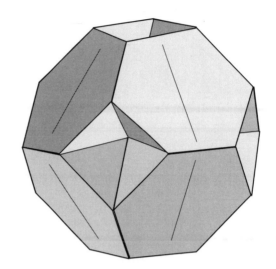

This is folded from an octahedron with sunken corners.

1

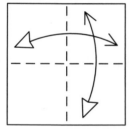

Fold and unfold.

2

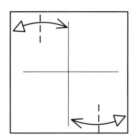

Fold and unfold, creasing lightly.

3

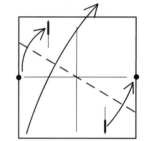

Align the dots and lines on the front and back.

4

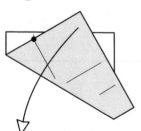

Unfold.

5

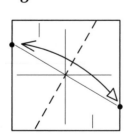

Fold and unfold. Rotate.

6

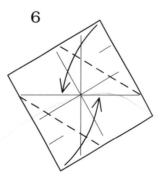

7

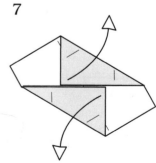

Unfold.

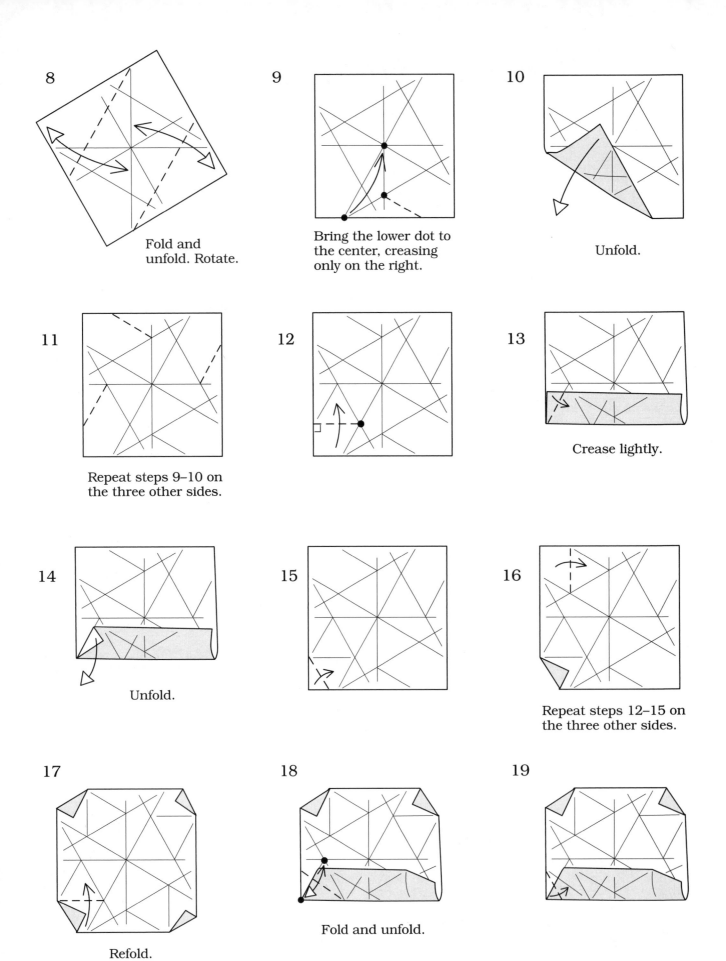

8 Fold and unfold. Rotate.

9 Bring the lower dot to the center, creasing only on the right.

10 Unfold.

11 Repeat steps 9–10 on the three other sides.

12

13 Crease lightly.

14 Unfold.

15

16 Repeat steps 12–15 on the three other sides.

17 Refold.

18 Fold and unfold.

19

20

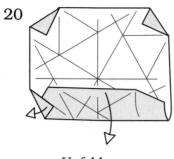

Unfold.

21

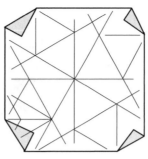

Repeat steps 17–20 on
the three other sides.

22

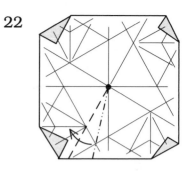

Push in at the dot.

23

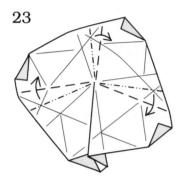

This is a view of the inside.
Rotate for each fold.

24

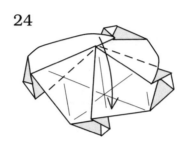

Flatten.

25

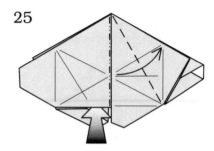

Repeat behind.

26

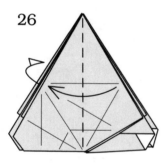

Repeat behind.

27

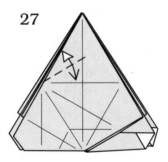

Fold and unfold
all the layers.

28

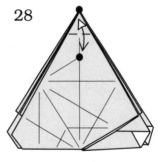

Fold and unfold.

29

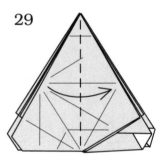

30

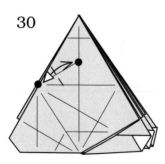

Fold and unfold
all the layers.

31

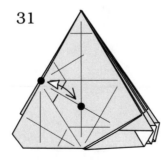

Fold and unfold.

32

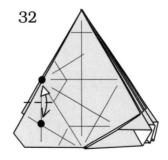

Fold and unfold.

33

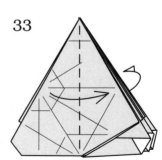

34

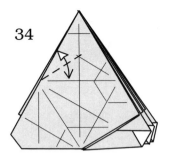

Fold and unfold.

35

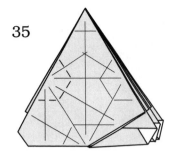

Repeat steps 30–32.

36

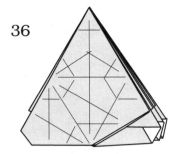

Repeat steps 33–35
two more times.

37

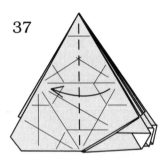

38

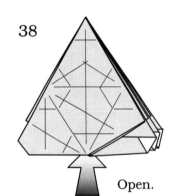

Open.

39

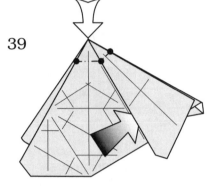

Note the dark arrow shows
the direction of the layers.
Sink, keeping the paper
locked at the dots.

40

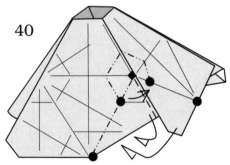

Form a sunken square by bringing the
pairs of dots together. Push in at the ◆.
Much of the paper will be tucked inside.

41

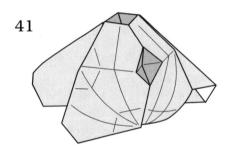

Repeat step 40 on the
three other sides.

42

Reverse-fold one
of the loose flaps
on the bottom.

43

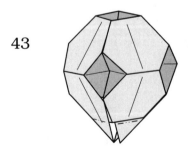

Continue reverse folding each of the layers
inside each other to form the bottom
sunken square. It is possible to inflate at
the bottom to round out this polyhedron.

44

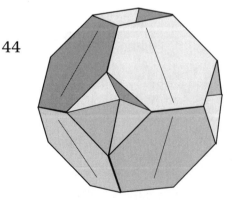

Dimpled Octahedron

Sunken Platonic Solids

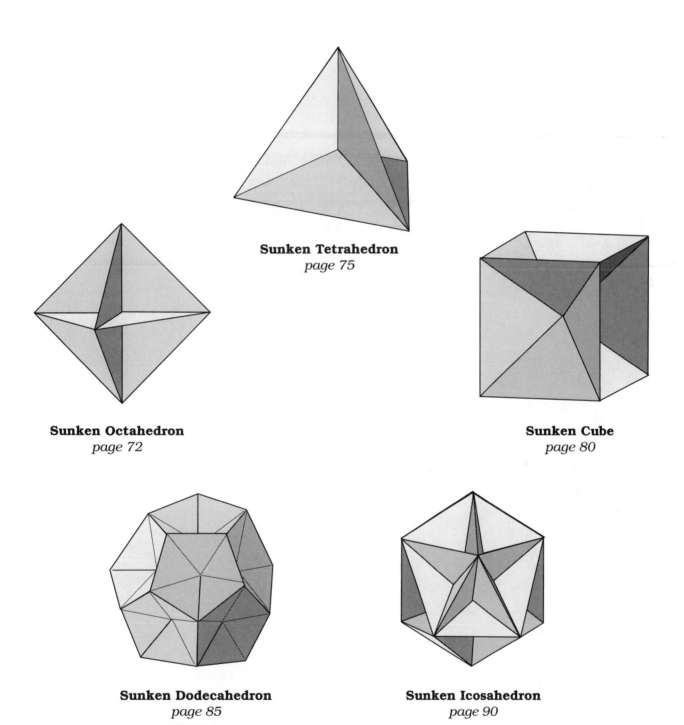

Sunken Tetrahedron
page 75

Sunken Octahedron
page 72

Sunken Cube
page 80

Sunken Dodecahedron
page 85

Sunken Icosahedron
page 90

This quintet makes for a beautiful and powerful
display. The folding methods for each of these
challenging models are amazingly different.

Sunken Octahedron

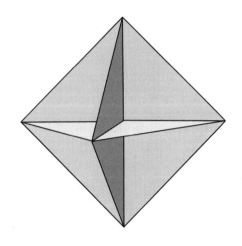

This model can be viewed as three intersecting squares correspond to the x, y, and z planes. A polyhedron with zero volume can be called a nolid ("not a solid"). This one would be an octahedral nolid.

1

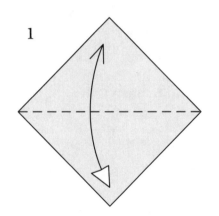

Fold and unfold.

2

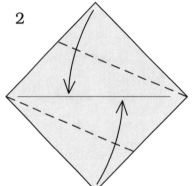

3

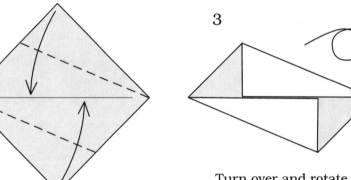

Turn over and rotate.

4

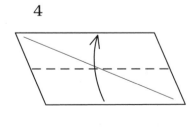

5

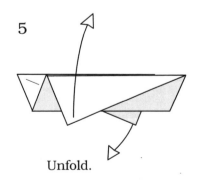

Unfold.

6

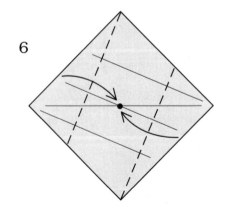

Rotate and repeat steps 2–4.

7

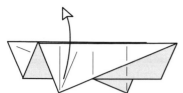

Lift up. Repeat
behind and rotate.

8

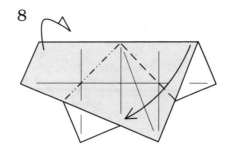

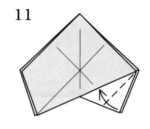

9

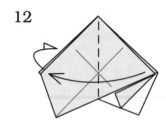

Unfold.

10

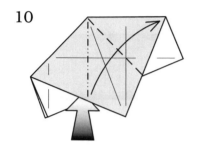

Squash-fold.

11

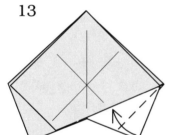

Turn over and repeat.

12

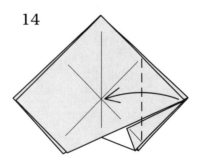

13

Turn over and repeat.

14

15

Tuck the top layer
underneath.

16

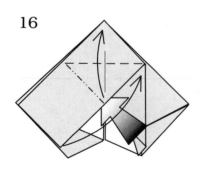

Squash-fold.

17

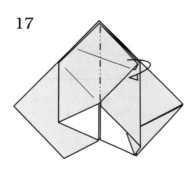

Tuck inside.

18

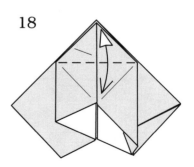

Fold and unfold.

19

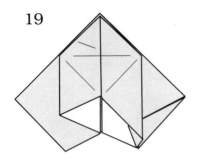

Turn over and
repeat steps 14–18.

20

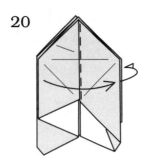

21

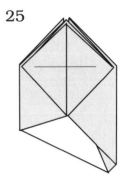

Tuck inside with
a reverse fold.

22

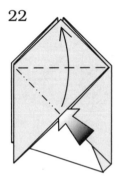

Squash-fold.

23

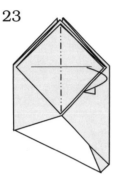

Tuck inside.

24

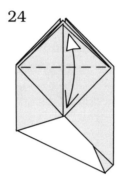

Fold and unfold.

25

Turn over and
repeat steps 21–24.

26

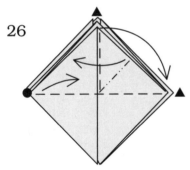

Bring the ▲'s together and lift
up at the dot. The model will
become three-dimensional.

27

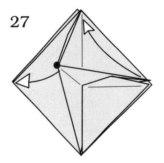

Unfold.

28

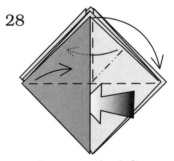

Open on the left
while tucking inside
the dark paper.

29

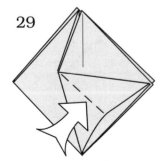

Snap shut.

30

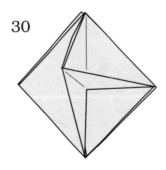

Repeat steps 26–29 on the
three remaining sides.

31

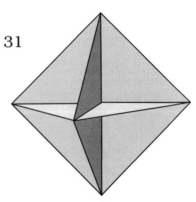

Sunken Octahedron

Sunken Tetrahedron

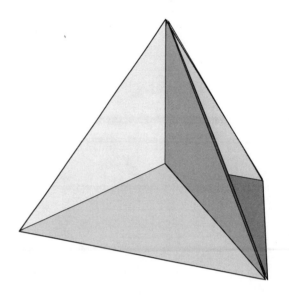

The sunken tetrahedron is composed of twelve isoceles triangles all meeting in the center. The sides of each triangle are proportional to 2√2, √3, √3. This can also be called a tetrahedral nolid.

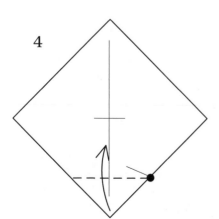

1

Fold and unfold.

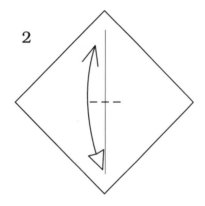

2

Fold and unfold creasing only at the center.

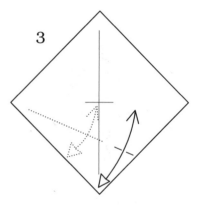

3

Kite fold and unfold creasing only on the right.

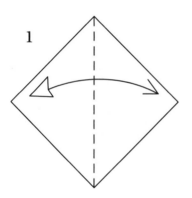

4

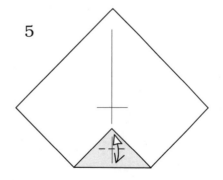

5

Fold and unfold.

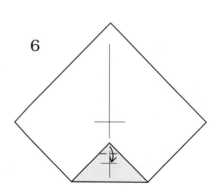

6

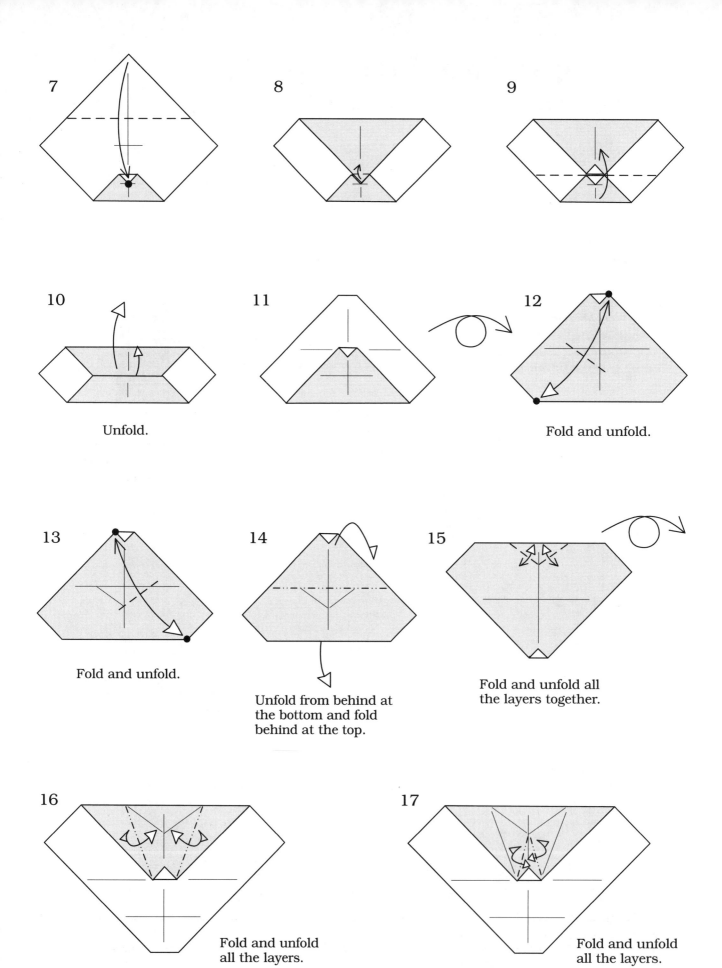

7

8

9

10

Unfold.

11

12

Fold and unfold.

13

Fold and unfold.

14

Unfold from behind at
the bottom and fold
behind at the top.

15

Fold and unfold all
the layers together.

16

Fold and unfold
all the layers.

17

Fold and unfold
all the layers.

18

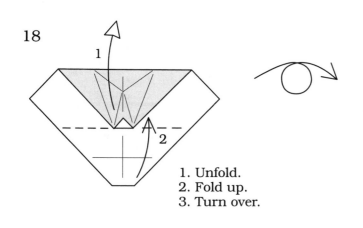

1. Unfold.
2. Fold up.
3. Turn over.

19

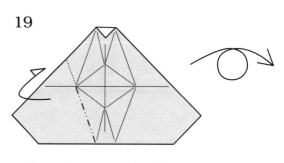

Do not crease at the top.

20

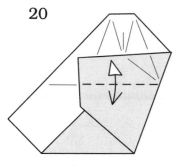

Fold and unfold
one layer.

21

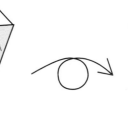

22

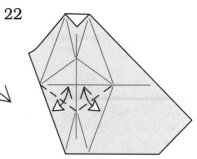

Fold and unfold
all layers.

23

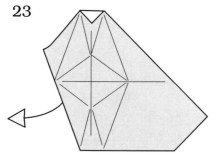

Unfold.

24

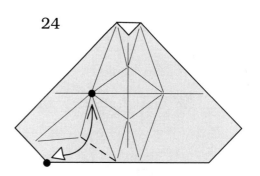

Fold and unfold.

25

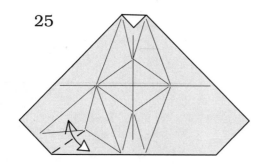

Fold and unfold.

26

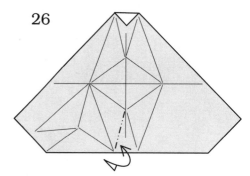

Fold and unfold.

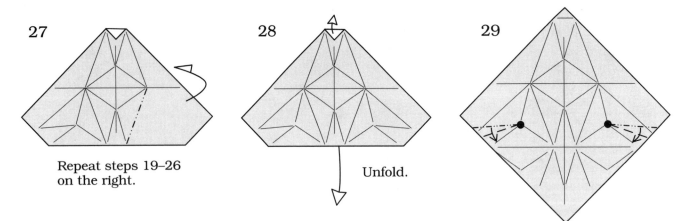

27

Repeat steps 19–26 on the right.

28

Unfold.

29

Push in at the dots. The model will become three-dimensional.

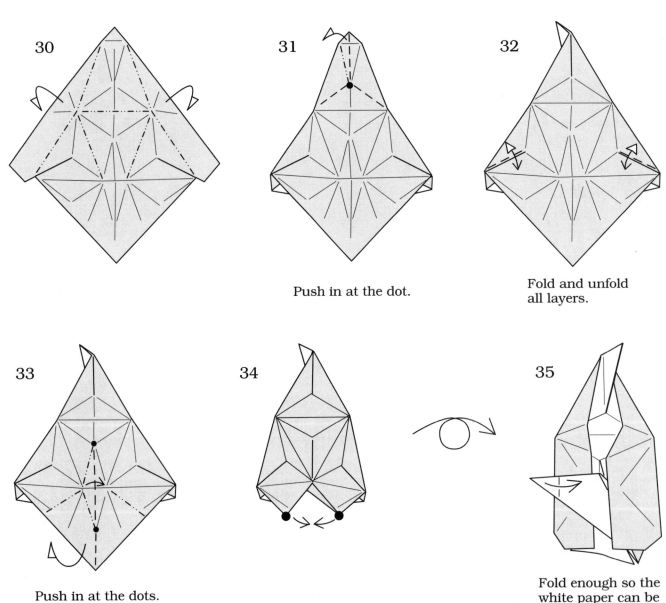

30

31

Push in at the dot.

32

Fold and unfold all layers.

33

Push in at the dots.

34

35

Fold enough so the white paper can be covered in step 36.

36

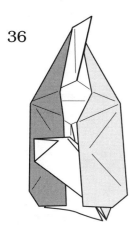

Bring the darker
paper to the front.

37

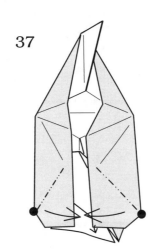

38

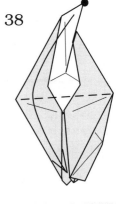

Tuck the dot inside.
Rotate so the dot is
at the top.

39

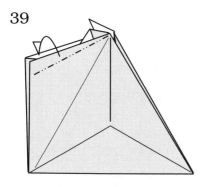

Fold all the layers together
except the last one.

40

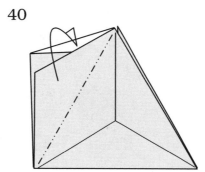

Tuck inside.

41

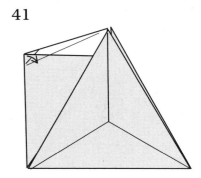

42

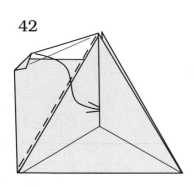

Tuck inside.

43

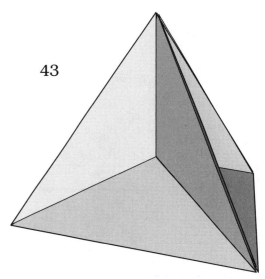

Sunken Tetrahedron

Sunken Cube

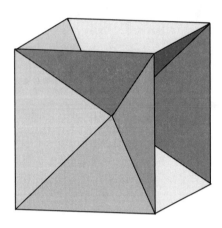

The sunken cube is composed of 24 isoceles triangles all meeting at the center. The sides of each triangle are proportional to 1, √3/2, √3/2. This beautiful shape can also be called a hexahedral nolid, that is, it comes from the cube but has no volume.

1

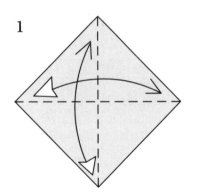

Fold and unfold along the diagonals.

2

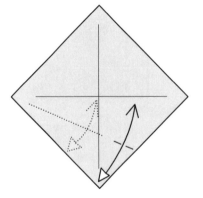

Kite fold and unfold creasing only on the right.

3

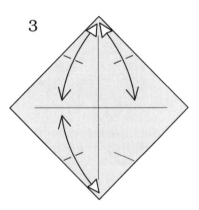

Repeat three more times.

4

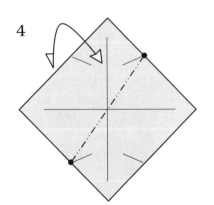

Fold and unfold.

5

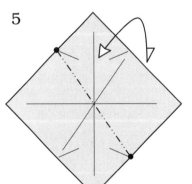

Fold and unfold.

6

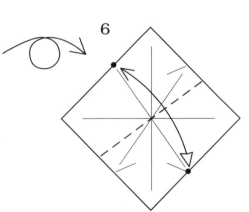

Fold and unfold.

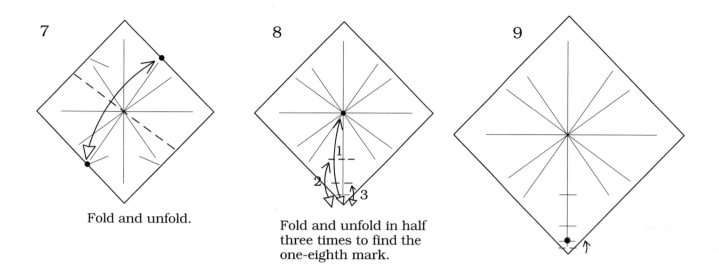

7 Fold and unfold.

8 Fold and unfold in half three times to find the one-eighth mark.

9

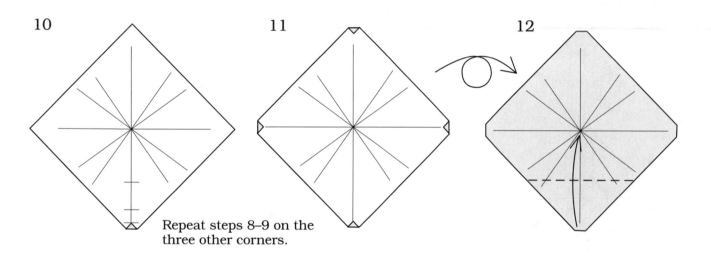

10 Repeat steps 8–9 on the three other corners.

11

12

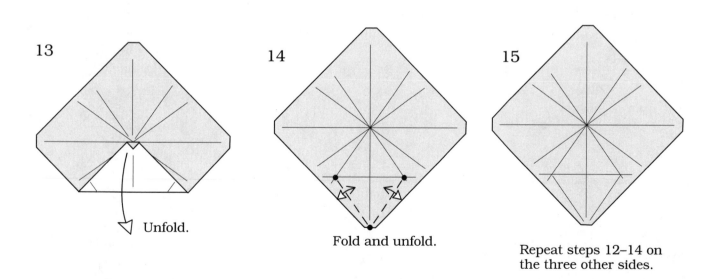

13 Unfold.

14 Fold and unfold.

15 Repeat steps 12–14 on the three other sides.

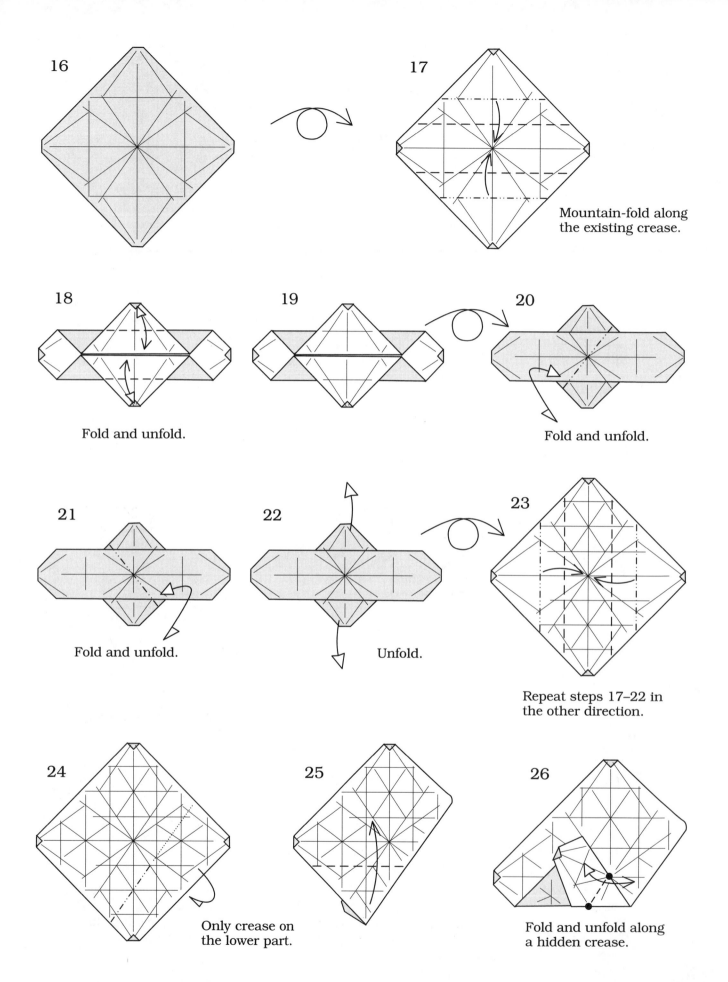

16

17

Mountain-fold along
the existing crease.

18

Fold and unfold.

19

20

Fold and unfold.

21

Fold and unfold.

22

Unfold.

23

Repeat steps 17–22 in
the other direction.

24

Only crease on
the lower part.

25

26

Fold and unfold along
a hidden crease.

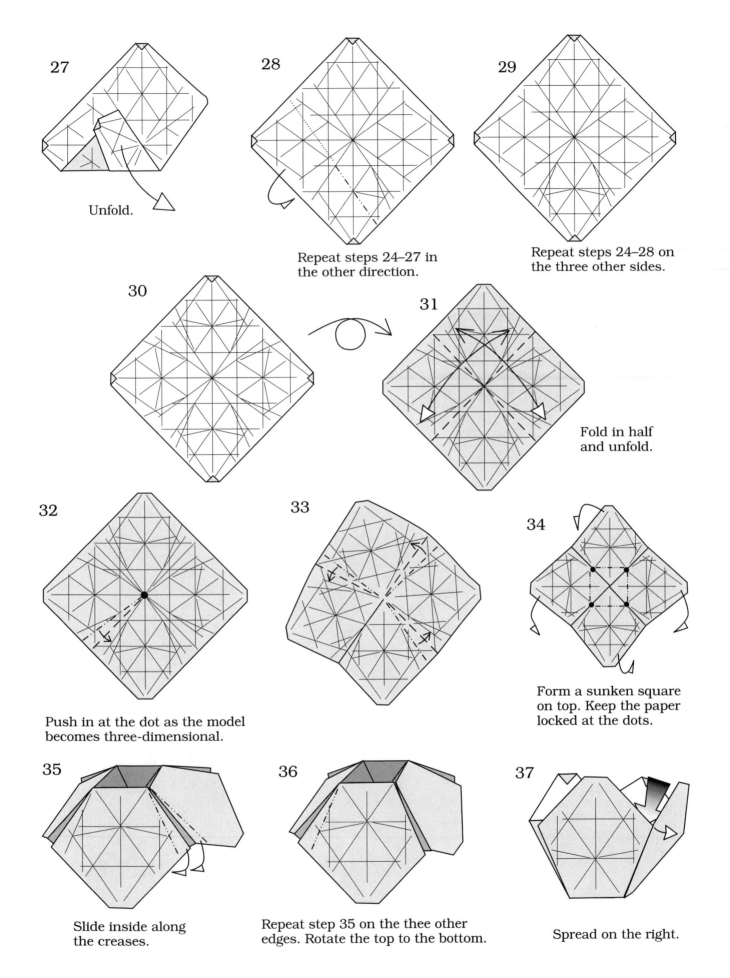

27

Unfold.

28

Repeat steps 24–27 in the other direction.

29

Repeat steps 24–28 on the three other sides.

30

31

Fold in half and unfold.

32

Push in at the dot as the model becomes three-dimensional.

33

34

Form a sunken square on top. Keep the paper locked at the dots.

35

Slide inside along the creases.

36

Repeat step 35 on the thee other edges. Rotate the top to the bottom.

37

Spread on the right.

Sunken Cube 83

38

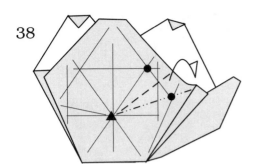

Mountain-fold along the existing crease. The dots will meet. Push in at the ▲.

39

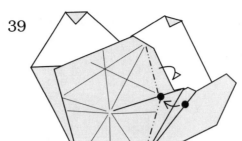

40

41

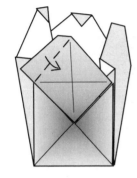

42

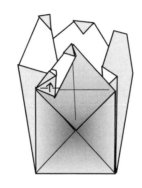

43

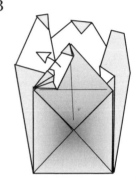

Unfold.

44

Repeat steps 37–43 on the three other sides.

45

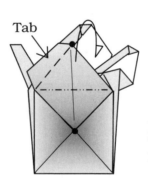

Tab

Fold inside as far as possible. The dots will meet inside. Note the tab on the left.

46

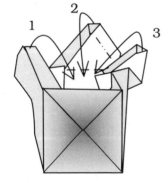

Continue folding inside in the order shown. For each of the three folds, cover the tabs. For the third fold, also tuck the tab inside.

47

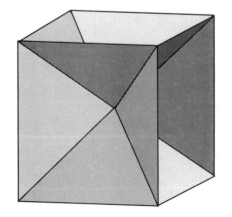

Sunken Cube

Sunken Dodecahedron

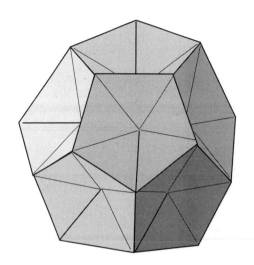

This sunken dodecahedron, one of several stellated icosahedrons, is composed of 60 equilateral triangles.

1

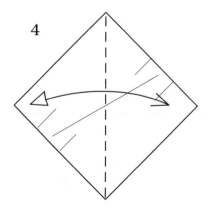

Fold and unfold to find the quarter marks.

2

Align the dots and lines on the front and back.

3

Unfold, turn over, and rotate.

4

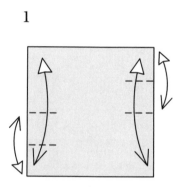

Fold and unfold.

5

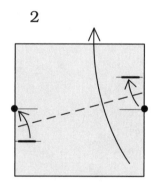

Fold and unfold.

6

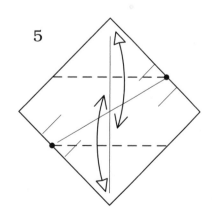

Fold and unfold.

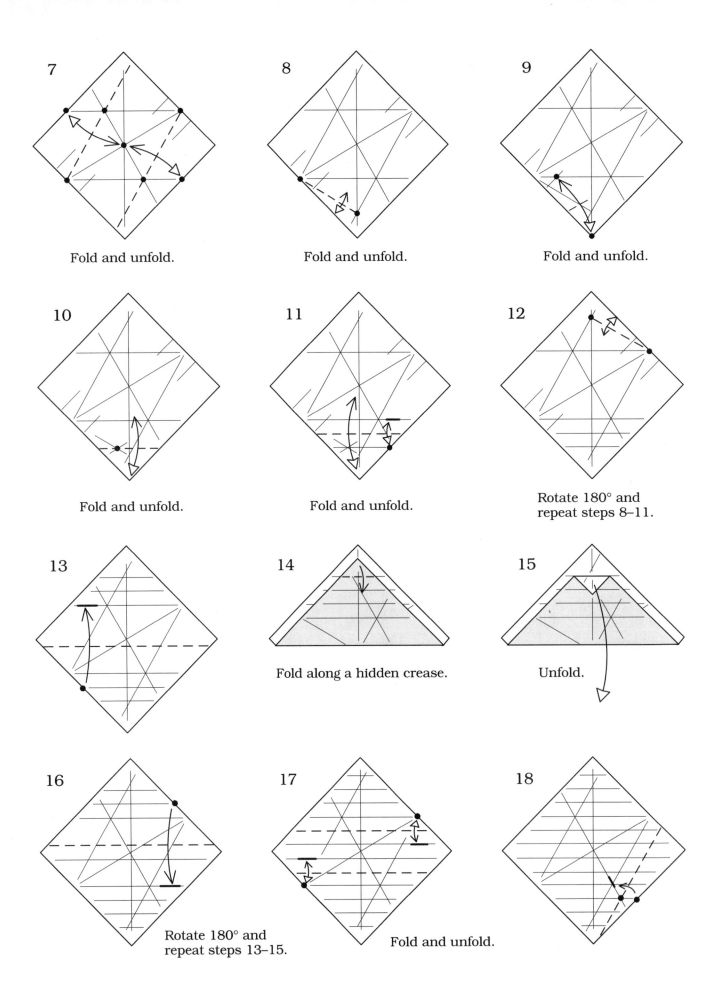

7

Fold and unfold.

8

Fold and unfold.

9

Fold and unfold.

10

Fold and unfold.

11

Fold and unfold.

12

Rotate 180° and repeat steps 8–11.

13

14

Fold along a hidden crease.

15

Unfold.

16

Rotate 180° and repeat steps 13–15.

17

Fold and unfold.

18

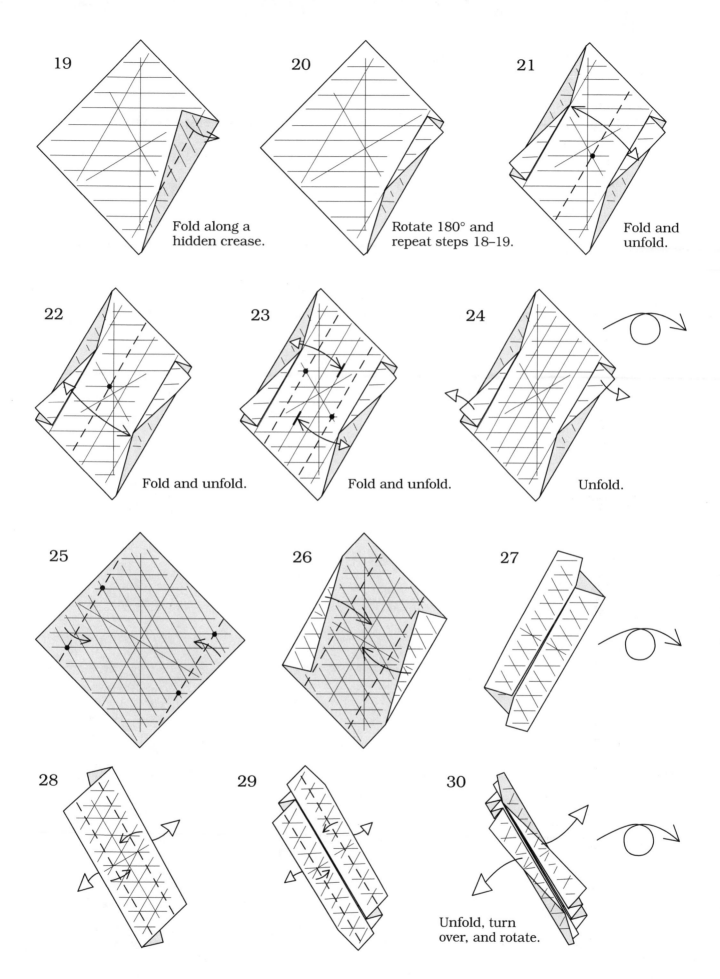

19 Fold along a hidden crease.

20 Rotate 180° and repeat steps 18–19.

21 Fold and unfold.

22 Fold and unfold.

23 Fold and unfold.

24 Unfold.

25

26

27

28

29

30 Unfold, turn over, and rotate.

Sunken Dodecahedron 87

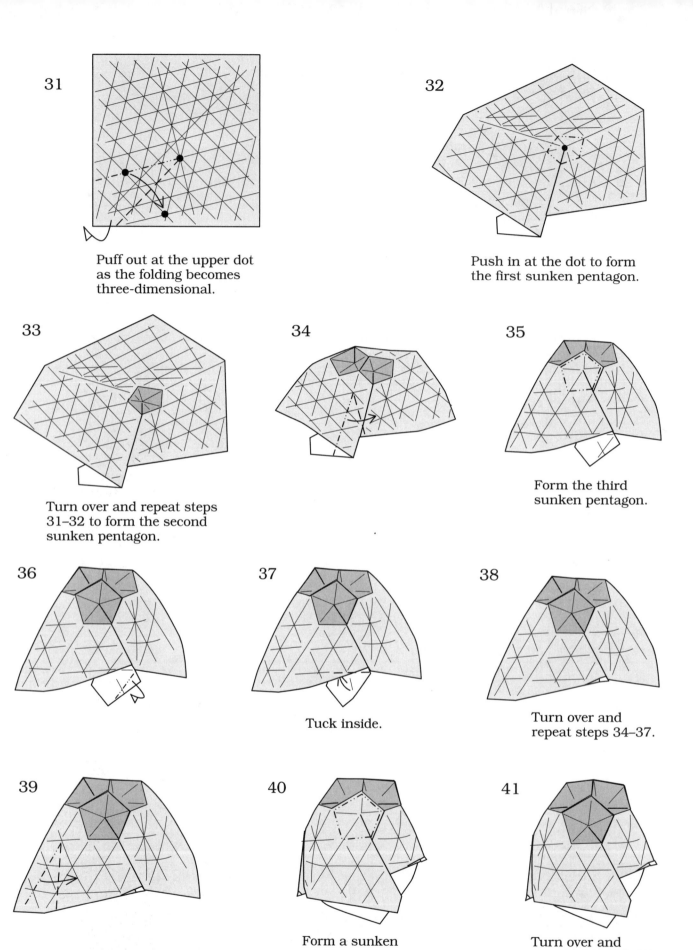

31 Puff out at the upper dot as the folding becomes three-dimensional.

32 Push in at the dot to form the first sunken pentagon.

33 Turn over and repeat steps 31–32 to form the second sunken pentagon.

34

35 Form the third sunken pentagon.

36

37 Tuck inside.

38 Turn over and repeat steps 34–37.

39

40 Form a sunken pentagon.

41 Turn over and repeat steps 39–40.

42

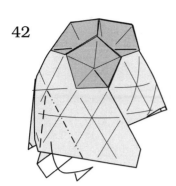

43

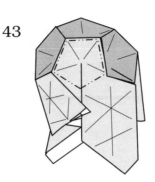

Form a sunken
pentagon.

44

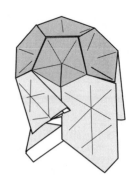

Turn over and repeat
steps 42–43. Rotate.

45

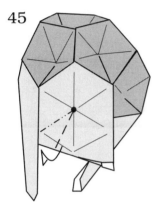

Push in at the dot. Form a
sunken pentagon and a tab.

46

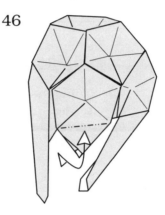

Fold and unfold.

47

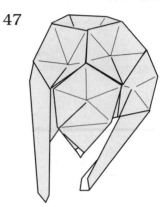

Turn over and repeat
steps 45–46. Rotate.

48

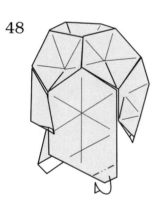

Fold a little bit behind.
Turn over and repeat.

49

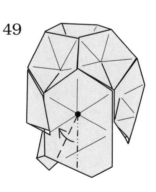

Push in at the dot to
form a sunken pentagon.
Turn over and repeat.

50

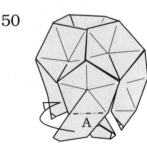

Region A meets the
one behind. Turn
over and repeat.

51

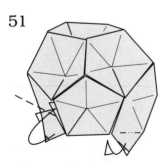

Tuck inside the pocket.
Repeat behind.

52

Sunken
Dodecahedron

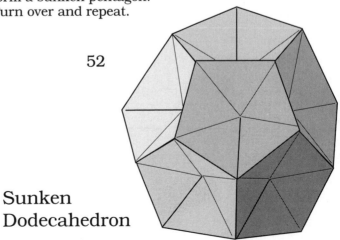

Sunken Icosahedron

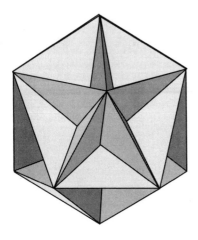

This complex shape is composed of 60 isoceles right triangles. It is formed by first making a fan. I gave it a four star (very complex) rating because of the sequence from steps 20–33 as the fan is turned into a tower. But the folds before and after are not so difficult.

Designing these polyhedra have been very rewarding. I hope you enjoy the techniques used to capture this seemingly impossible shape.

1

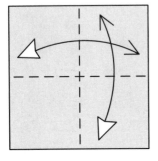

Fold and unfold.

2

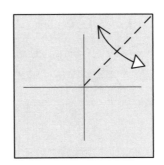

Fold and unfold.

3

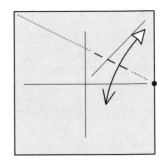

Fold and unfold, creasing only along the diagonal.

4

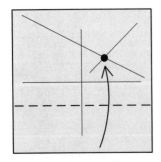

This divides the paper in thirds.

5

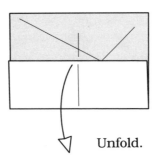

Unfold.

6

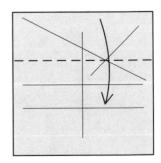

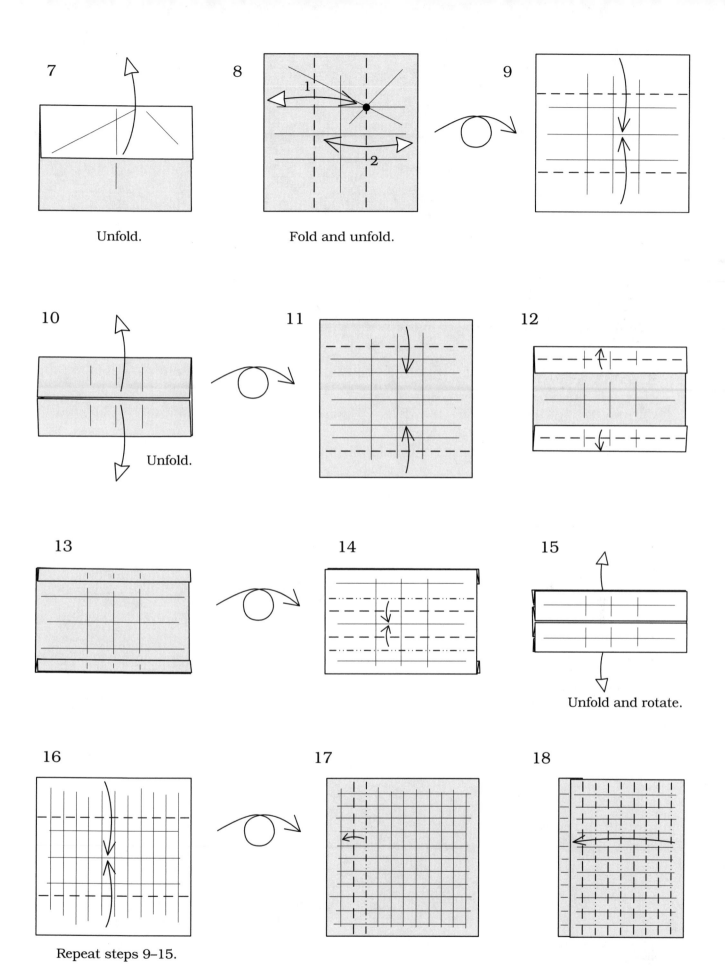

7

Unfold.

8

Fold and unfold.

9

10

Unfold.

11

12

13

14

15

Unfold and rotate.

16

Repeat steps 9–15.

17

18

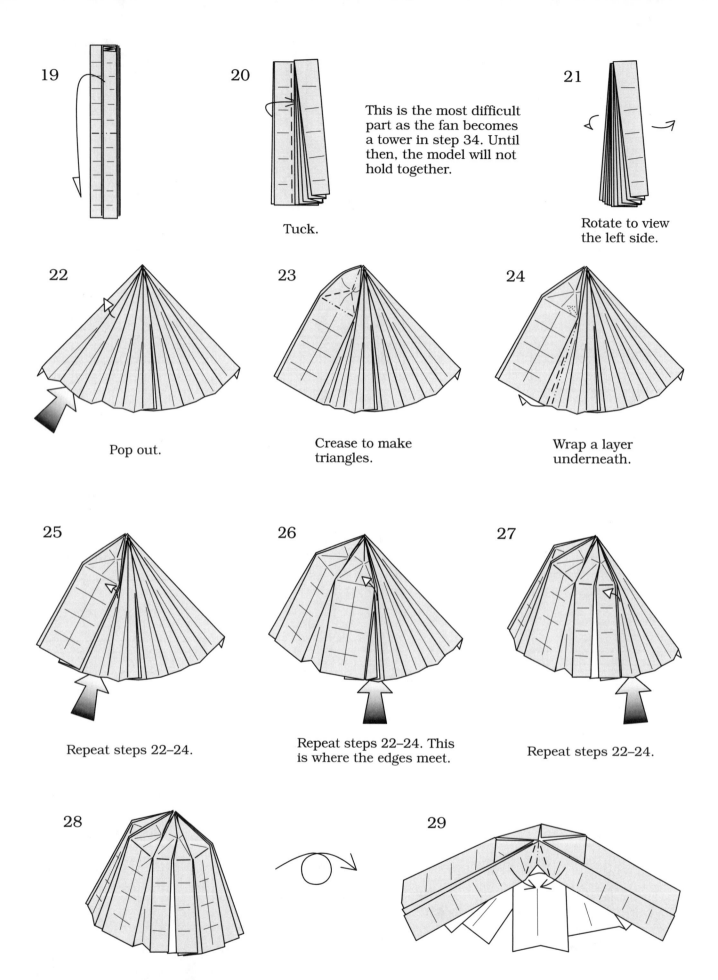

19

20

Tuck.

This is the most difficult part as the fan becomes a tower in step 34. Until then, the model will not hold together.

21

Rotate to view the left side.

22

Pop out.

23

Crease to make triangles.

24

Wrap a layer underneath.

25

Repeat steps 22–24.

26

Repeat steps 22–24. This is where the edges meet.

27

Repeat steps 22–24.

28

29

30

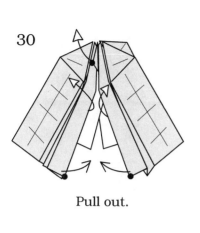

Pull out.

31

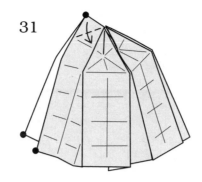

32

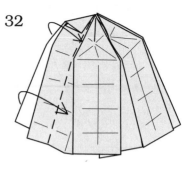

Tuck inside.

33

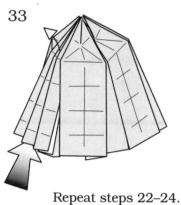

Repeat steps 22–24.

Finally, the fan has turned into a tower. Hopefully, the model should be able to hold together.

34

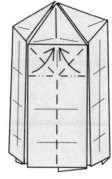

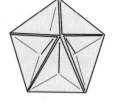

View of top.

Bring the edges together and then let go.

35

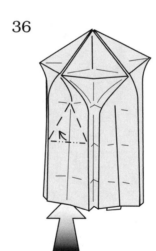

Repeat step 34 four more times going around.

36

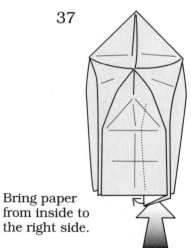

37

Bring paper from inside to the right side.

38

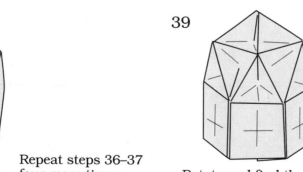

Repeat steps 36–37 four more times going around.

39

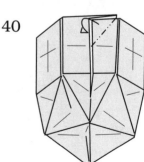

Rotate and find the side with the edge showing.

40

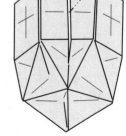

41

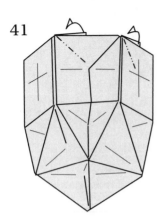

Fold all the loose edges
going all around.

42

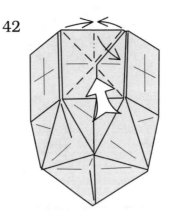

Form a sunken triangle
bringing the extra
paper to the front.

43

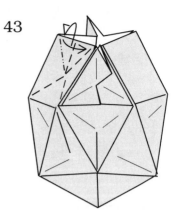

Form a sunken triangle
while folding the extra
paper inside.

44

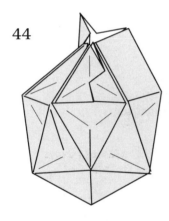

Repeat steps 43
on the right.

45

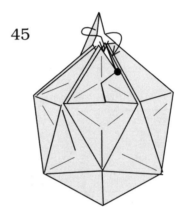

Form the last two triangles on the
back while bringing the extra paper
to the front inside the front triangle.

46

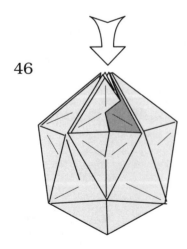

Bring the dark paper to the front
to lock the folds. Also push down
to keep the folds in place.

47

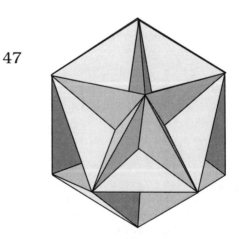

Sunken Icosahedron

Dodecahedra

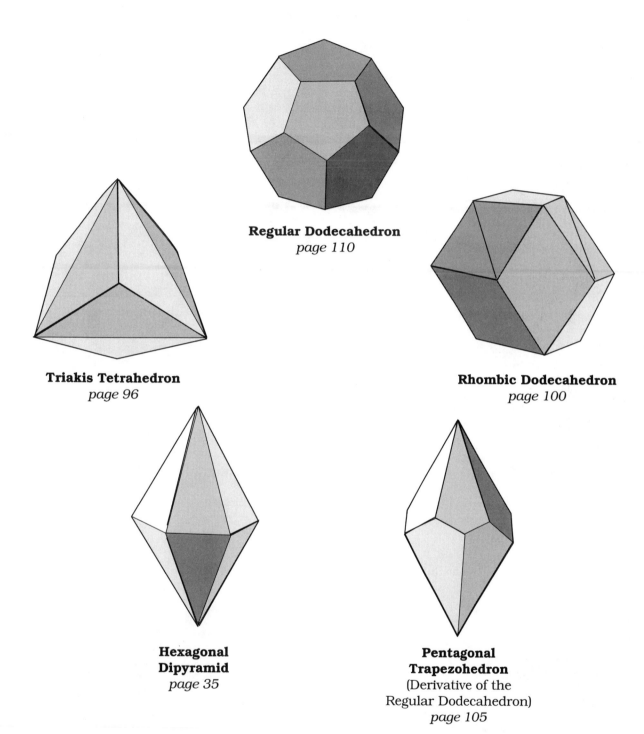

Regular Dodecahedron
page 110

Triakis Tetrahedron
page 96

Rhombic Dodecahedron
page 100

**Hexagonal
Dipyramid**
page 35

**Pentagonal
Trapezohedron**
(Derivative of the
Regular Dodecahedron)
page 105

Dodecahedra are polyhedra with twelve sides. Most of these
are quite challenging to fold. The regular dodecahedron is a
Platonic solid composed of twelve pentagons. The pentagonal
trapezohedron has ten sides, though the folding is related to
the regular dodecahedron.

Triakis Tetrahedron

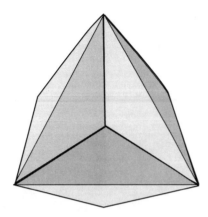

This puffed-out
tetrahedron is composed
of twelve isoceles triangles.

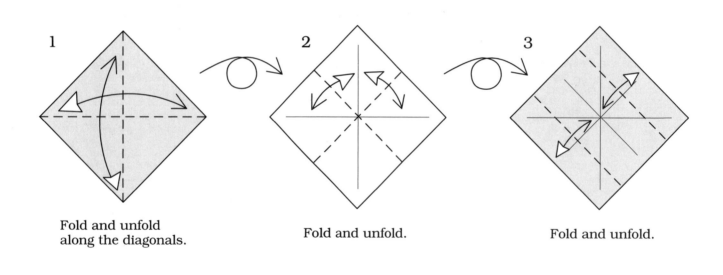

1 Fold and unfold
along the diagonals.

2 Fold and unfold.

3 Fold and unfold.

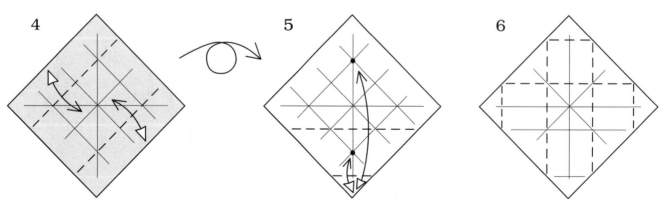

4 Fold and unfold.

5 Fold and unfold.

6 Repeat steps 4–5 on the
three remaining sides.

7

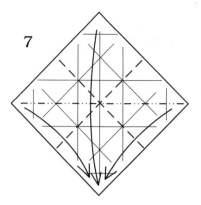

Bring the four
corners together.

8

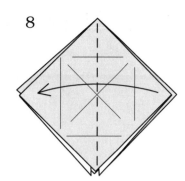

9

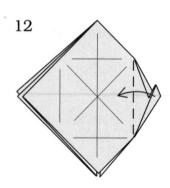

Fold and unfold,
creasing lightly.

10

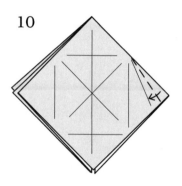

11

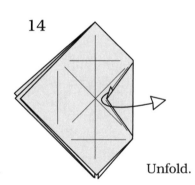

Squash-fold.

12

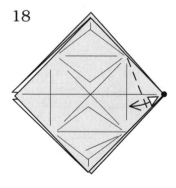

13

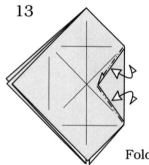

Fold and unfold.

14

Unfold.

15

16

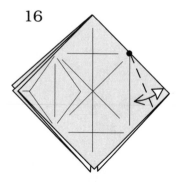

Repeat steps 9–15
three more times.

17

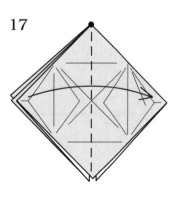

Fold one layer and rotate
the dot to the right.

18

Repeat steps 9–14, folding
all the layers together.

Triakis Tetrahedron 97

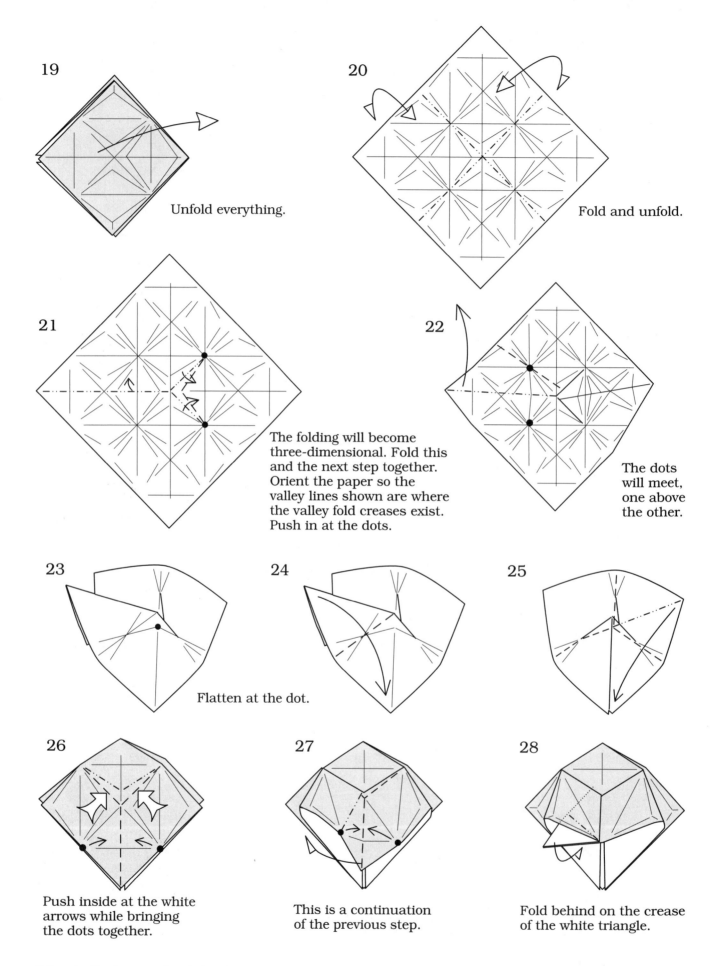

19

Unfold everything.

20

Fold and unfold.

21

The folding will become three-dimensional. Fold this and the next step together. Orient the paper so the valley lines shown are where the valley fold creases exist. Push in at the dots.

22

The dots will meet, one above the other.

23

24

Flatten at the dot.

25

26

Push inside at the white arrows while bringing the dots together.

27

This is a continuation of the previous step.

28

Fold behind on the crease of the white triangle.

29

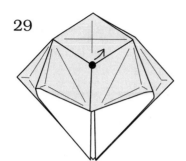

Puff out at the dot.

30

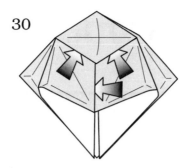

Note the orientation
of the three pockets.

31

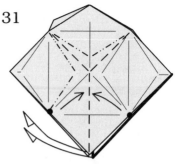

Repeat steps 26–27
while including the flap
behind on the right.

32

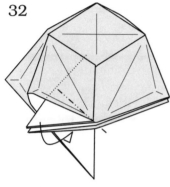

Fold both layers
behind on the crease.

33

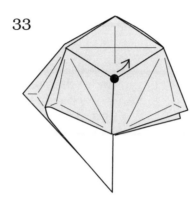

Puff out at the dot.

34

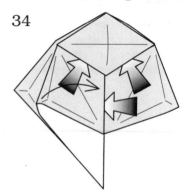

Note the three pockets.
Open on the left, or rotate.

35

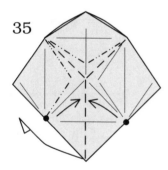

Repeat steps 26–30.

36

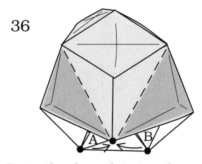

1. Bring the three dots together and
2. flatten the dark triangles while
3. keeping the the triangles A and B
   (and C hidden) in the center of the
   model, not between the dark triangles.
Do this all around.

37

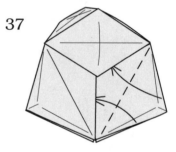

Tuck inside.

38

Adjust the creases.

39

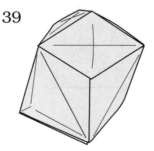

Repeat steps 37–38 two more
times. It is possible to inflate this.
The model is rotated to stand.

40

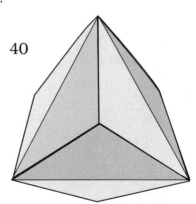

Triakis Tetrahedron

Triakis Tetrahedron 99

Rhombic Dodecahedron

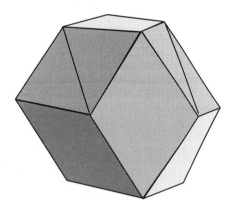

This beautiful polyhedron is composed of twelve diamonds. The ratio of the diagonals on each side is 1 by √2. At some vertices, four sides meet, at others three sides meet.

1

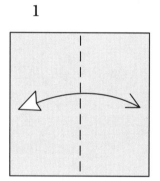

Fold and unfold.

2

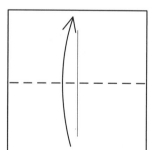

3

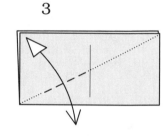

Fold and unfold one layer.

4

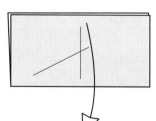

Unfold and rotate.

5

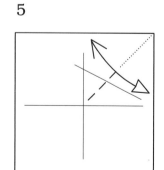

Fold and unfold creasing at the intersection.

6

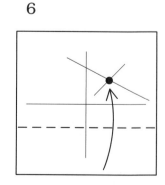

This divides the paper in thirds.

7

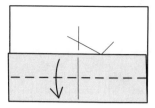

8

9

10

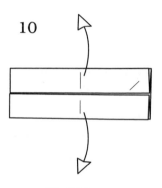

Unfold.

11

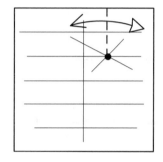

Fold, unfold
and rotate.

12

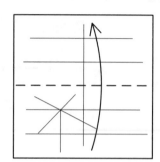

13

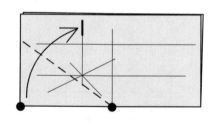

Fold the lower left corner
to the crease line.

14

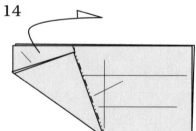

15

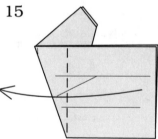

16

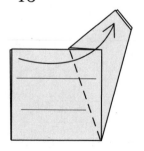

17

18

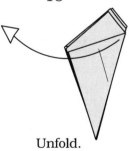

Unfold.

19

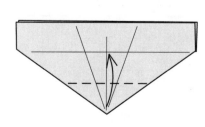

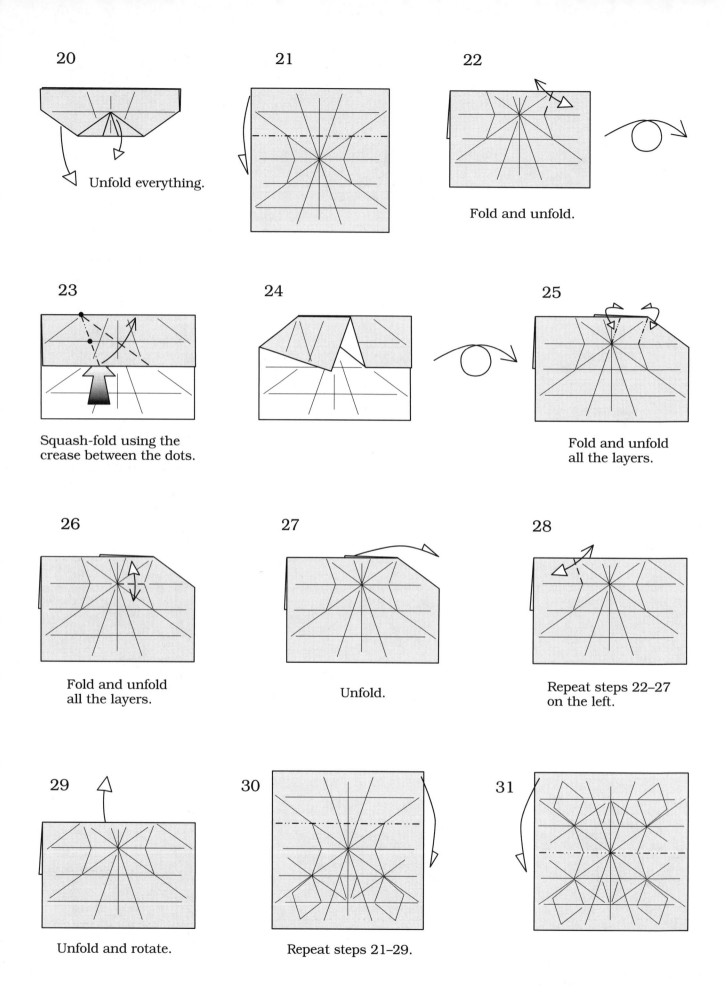

20

Unfold everything.

21

22

Fold and unfold.

23

Squash-fold using the crease between the dots.

24

25

Fold and unfold all the layers.

26

Fold and unfold all the layers.

27

Unfold.

28

Repeat steps 22–27 on the left.

29

Unfold and rotate.

30

Repeat steps 21–29.

31

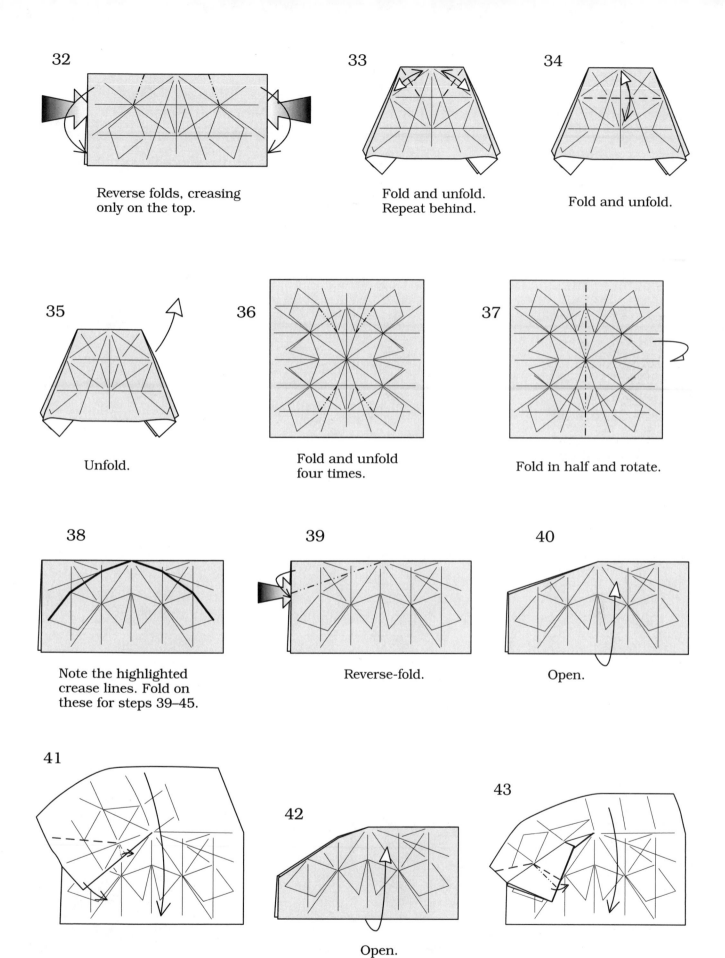

32

Reverse folds, creasing
only on the top.

33

Fold and unfold.
Repeat behind.

34

Fold and unfold.

35

Unfold.

36

Fold and unfold
four times.

37

Fold in half and rotate.

38

Note the highlighted
crease lines. Fold on
these for steps 39–45.

39

Reverse-fold.

40

Open.

41

42

Open.

43

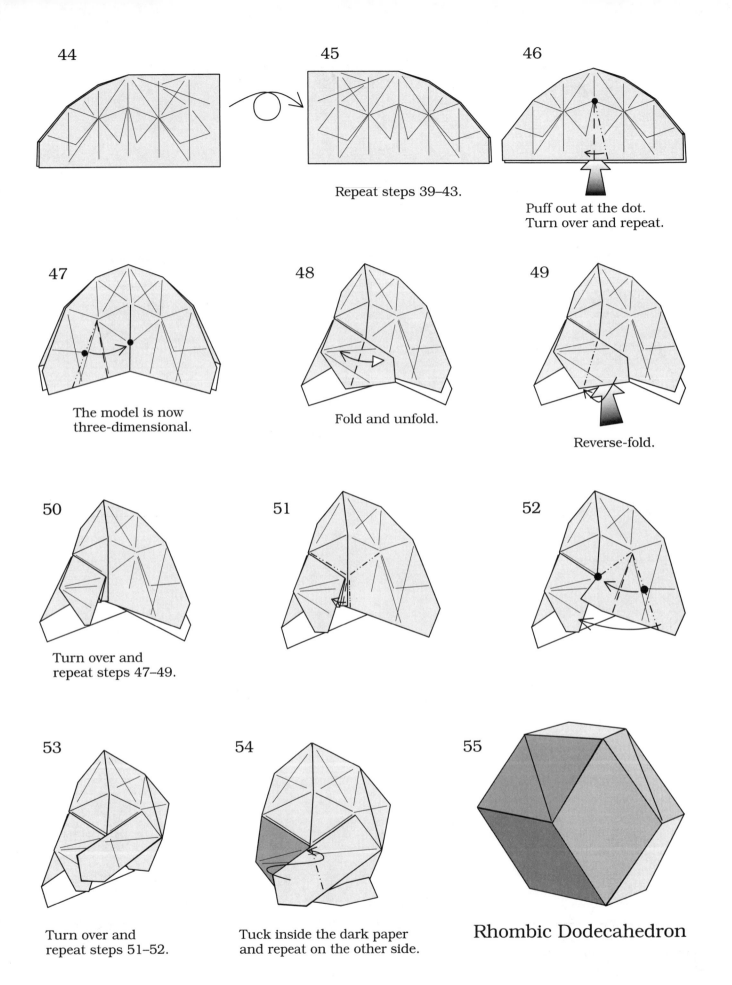

44

45

Repeat steps 39–43.

46

Puff out at the dot.
Turn over and repeat.

47

The model is now
three-dimensional.

48

Fold and unfold.

49

Reverse-fold.

50

Turn over and
repeat steps 47–49.

51

52

53

Turn over and
repeat steps 51–52.

54

Tuck inside the dark paper
and repeat on the other side.

55

Rhombic Dodecahedron

Pentagonal Trapezohedron

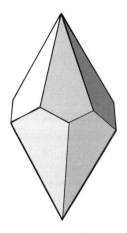

This trapezohedron, or antidiamond, is composed of ten quadrilaterals. In each quadrilateral, three of the angles are 108° and one is 36°. The pentagons of the regular dodecahedron also have angles of 108°, relating these two polyhedra—if the top and bottom of this shape were chopped off, it would form a dodecahedron.

This model begins by folding a 36° line going through the center. I thank Robert Lang for working out a method to achieve this.

1

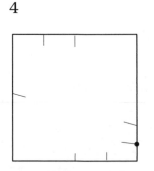

Fold in half on two sides, making small marks.

2

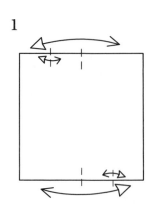

Fold and unfold making small marks on the left and right.

3

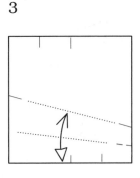

Creasing very lightly or not at all, bring the bottom edge to the line. Crease only on the right.

4

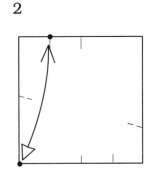

All the folding done so far was to locate the mark with the dot. Rotate 180°.

5

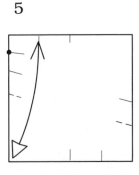

Repeat steps 2–3.

6

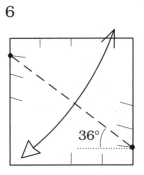

Fold and unfold. This is the first real fold.

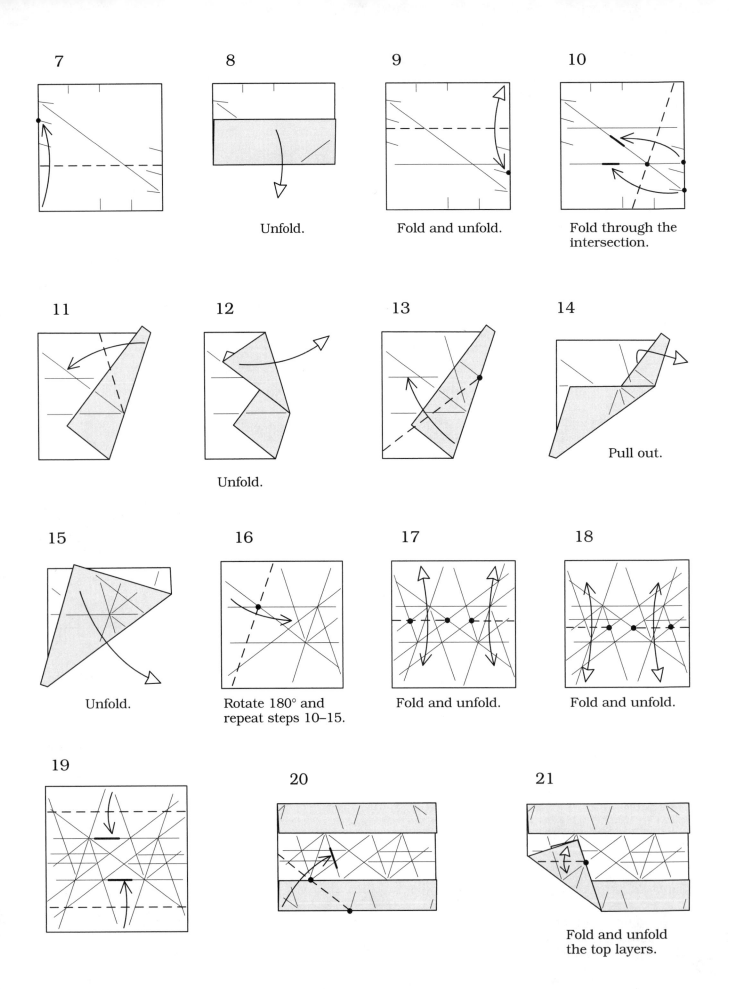

7

8

Unfold.

9

Fold and unfold.

10

Fold through the intersection.

11

12

Unfold.

13

14

Pull out.

15

Unfold.

16

Rotate 180° and repeat steps 10–15.

17

Fold and unfold.

18

Fold and unfold.

19

20

21

Fold and unfold the top layers.

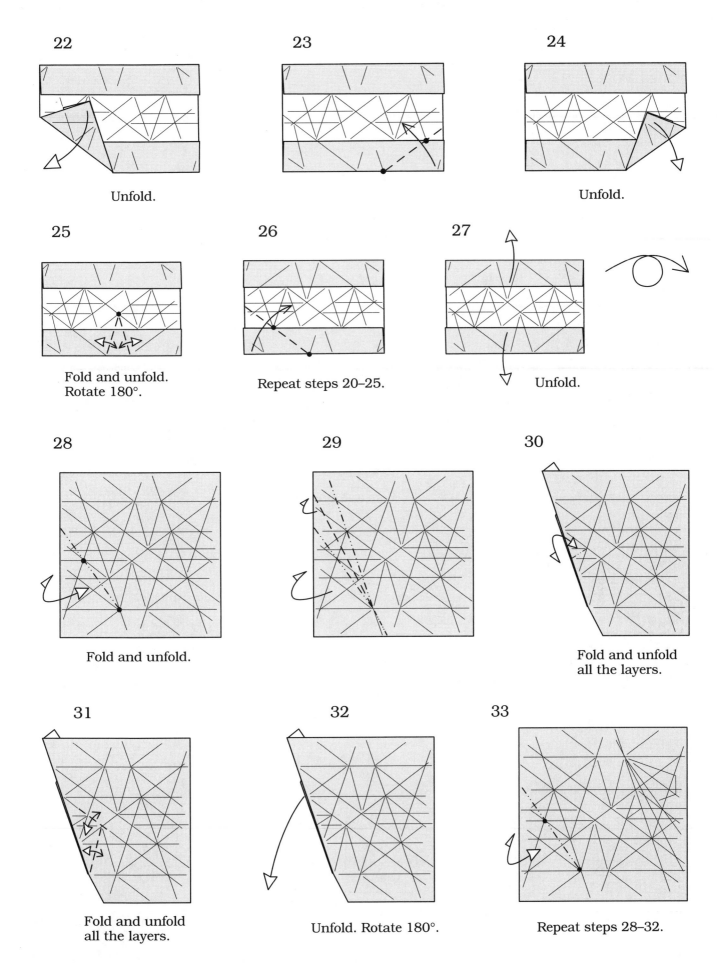

22

Unfold.

23

24

Unfold.

25

Fold and unfold.
Rotate 180°.

26

Repeat steps 20–25.

27

Unfold.

28

Fold and unfold.

29

30

Fold and unfold
all the layers.

31

Fold and unfold
all the layers.

32

Unfold. Rotate 180°.

33

Repeat steps 28–32.

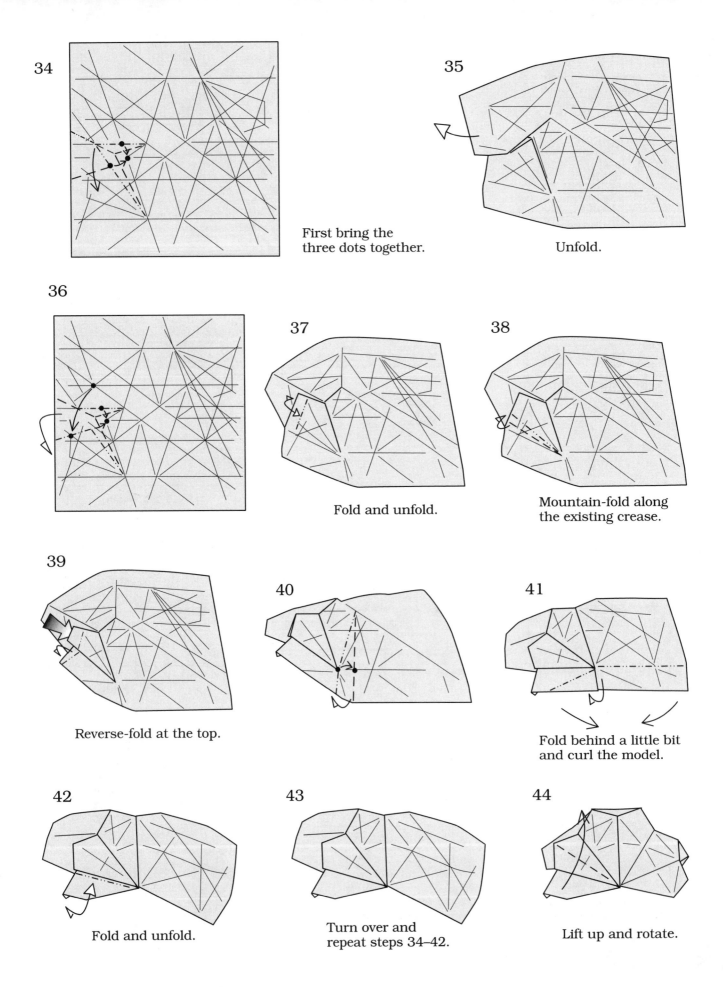

34

First bring the
three dots together.

35

Unfold.

36

37

Fold and unfold.

38

Mountain-fold along
the existing crease.

39

Reverse-fold at the top.

40

41

Fold behind a little bit
and curl the model.

42

Fold and unfold.

43

Turn over and
repeat steps 34–42.

44

Lift up and rotate.

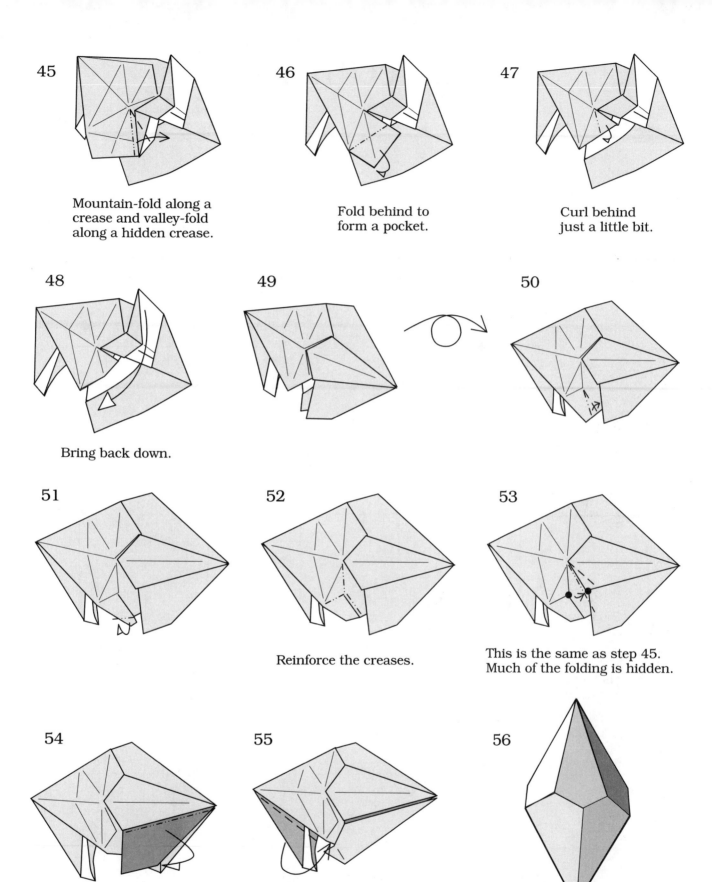

45

Mountain-fold along a
crease and valley-fold
along a hidden crease.

46

Fold behind to
form a pocket.

47

Curl behind
just a little bit.

48

Bring back down.

49

50

51

52

Reinforce the creases.

53

This is the same as step 45.
Much of the folding is hidden.

54

Tuck the dark flap
into the pocket.

55

Tuck the dark flap
into the pocket.

56

Pentagonal
Trapezohedron

Dodecahedron

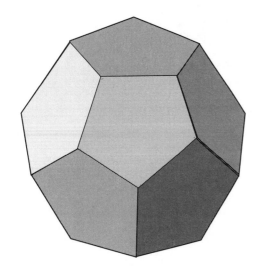

To Plato, this dodecahedron, the quintessence (the "fifth being"), represented the whole universe.

In designing this, I certainly had to dig quite deeply. I hope you, too, enjoy the magic of the dodecahedron.

1

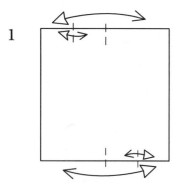

Fold in half on two sides, making small marks.

2

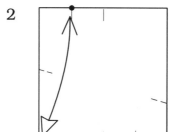

Fold and unfold making small marks on the left and right.

3

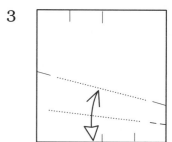

Creasing very lightly or not at all, bring the bottom edge to the line. Crease only on the right.

4

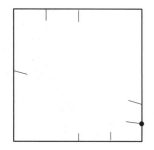

All the folding done so far was to locate the mark with the dot. Rotate 180°.

5

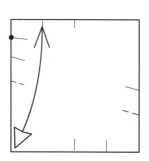

Repeat steps 2–3.

6

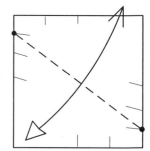

Fold and unfold. This is the first real fold.

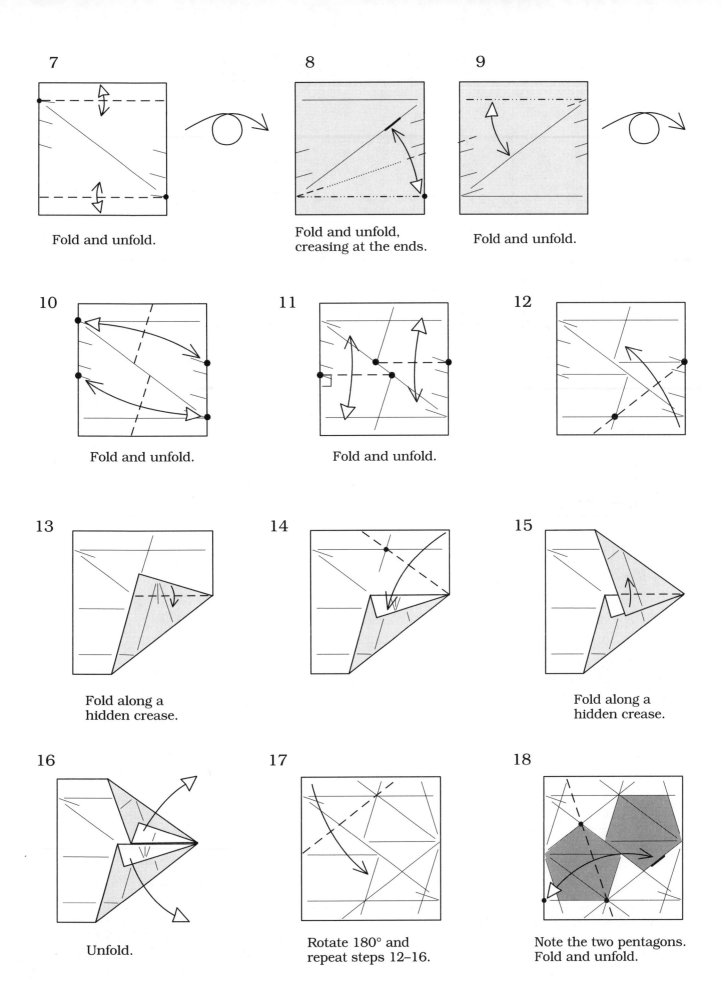

7

Fold and unfold.

8

Fold and unfold, creasing at the ends.

9

Fold and unfold.

10

Fold and unfold.

11

Fold and unfold.

12

13

Fold along a hidden crease.

14

15

Fold along a hidden crease.

16

Unfold.

17

Rotate 180° and repeat steps 12–16.

18

Note the two pentagons. Fold and unfold.

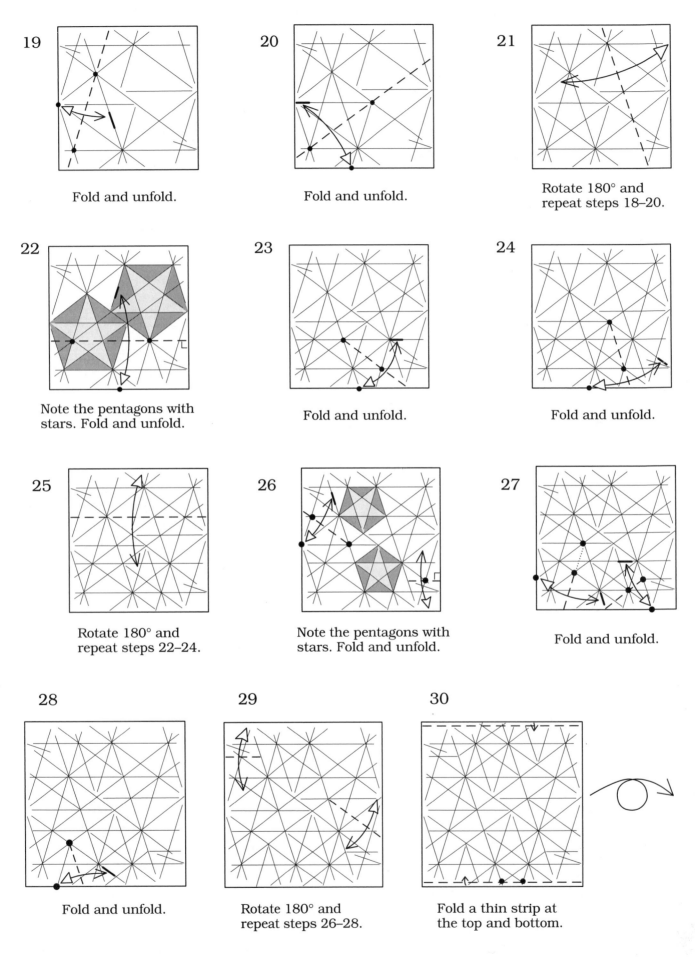

19 Fold and unfold.

20 Fold and unfold.

21 Rotate 180° and repeat steps 18–20.

22 Note the pentagons with stars. Fold and unfold.

23 Fold and unfold.

24 Fold and unfold.

25 Rotate 180° and repeat steps 22–24.

26 Note the pentagons with stars. Fold and unfold.

27 Fold and unfold.

28 Fold and unfold.

29 Rotate 180° and repeat steps 26–28.

30 Fold a thin strip at the top and bottom.

31

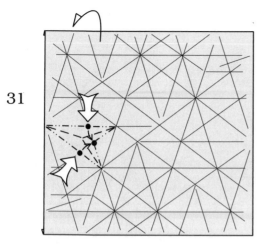

The folding will become three-dimensional.
Bring the three dots together.

32

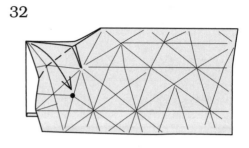

33

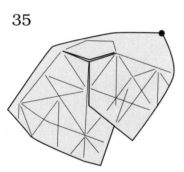

Unfold.

34

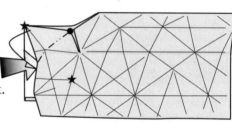

Push in at the dot.
The ★'s will meet
inside. Rotate the
dot to the center.

35

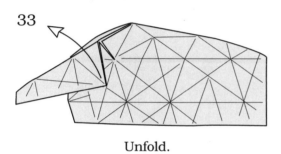

Rotate the dot to the front
and repeat steps 31–34.

36

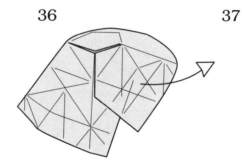

Unfold everything.

37

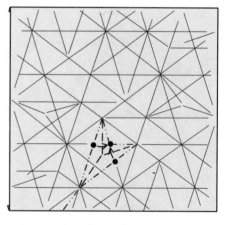

Bring the three dots together.
The model will become
three-dimensional again.

38

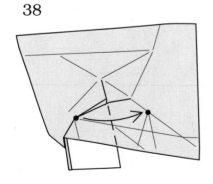

39

Turn over and
repeat steps 37–38.

40

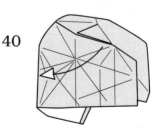

Unfold everything.

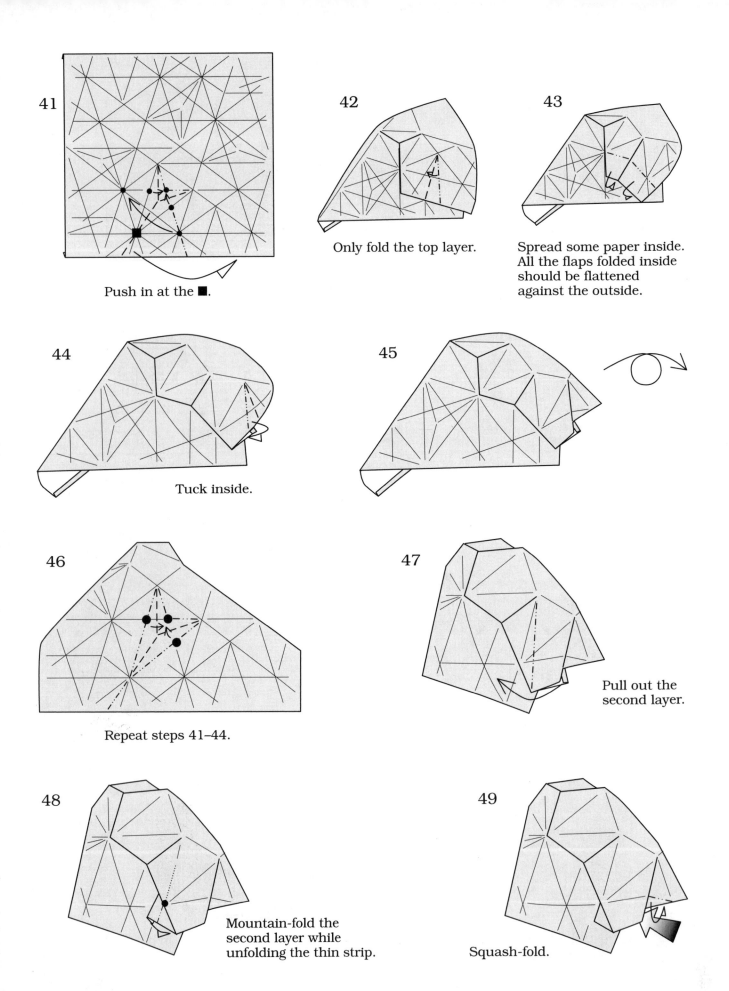

41 Push in at the ■.

42 Only fold the top layer.

43 Spread some paper inside. All the flaps folded inside should be flattened against the outside.

44 Tuck inside.

45

46 Repeat steps 41–44.

47 Pull out the second layer.

48 Mountain-fold the second layer while unfolding the thin strip.

49 Squash-fold.

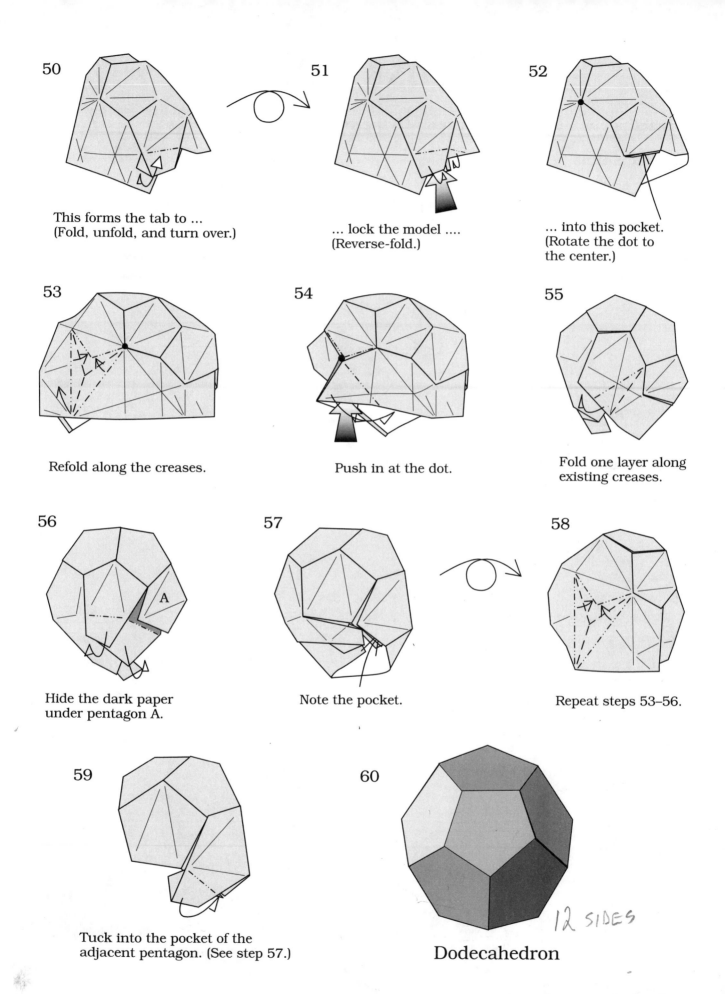

50

This forms the tab to ...
(Fold, unfold, and turn over.)

51

... lock the model ....
(Reverse-fold.)

52

... into this pocket.
(Rotate the dot to
the center.)

53

Refold along the creases.

54

Push in at the dot.

55

Fold one layer along
existing creases.

56

A

Hide the dark paper
under pentagon A.

57

Note the pocket.

58

Repeat steps 53–56.

59

Tuck into the pocket of the
adjacent pentagon. (See step 57.)

60

12 SIDES

Dodecahedron

Crease Patterns

Polyhedra composed of equilateral triangles:

Platonic Solids

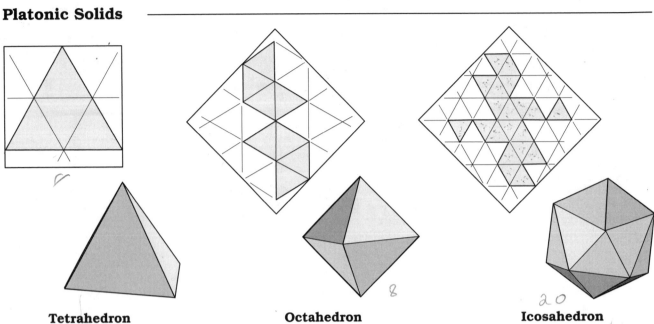

Tetrahedron	Octahedron	Icosahedron

Other

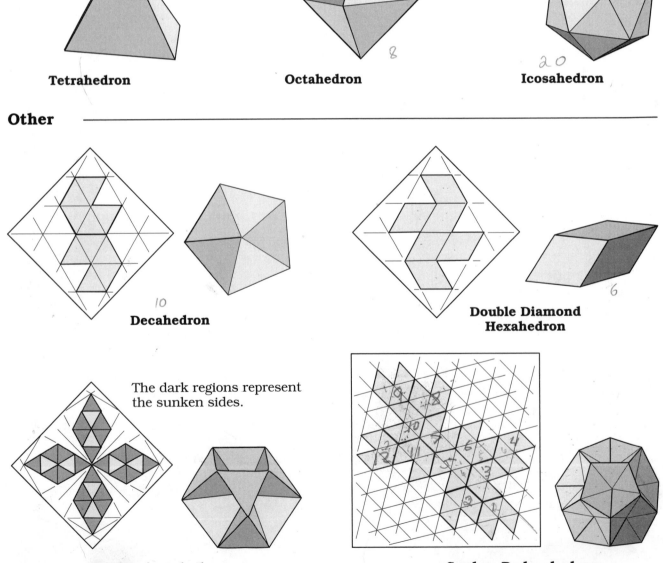

Decahedron

Double Diamond
Hexahedron

The dark regions represent
the sunken sides.

Octahemioctahedron

Sunken Dodecahedron

Polyhedra not composed of equilateral triangles:
Prisms

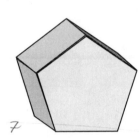

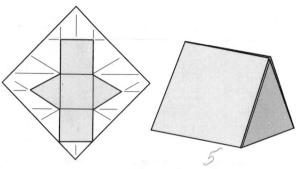

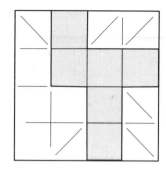

Triangular Prism

Cube

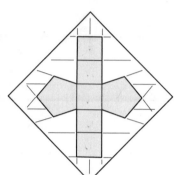

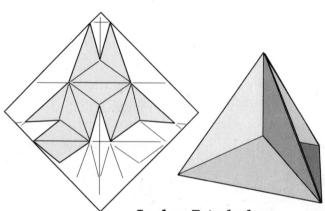

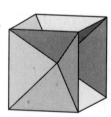

Pentagonal Prism

Hexagonal Prism

Other

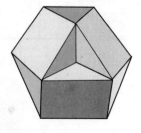

Sunken Tetrahedron

Sunken Cube

The dark regions
represent the sunken
triangles at one side.

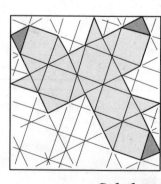

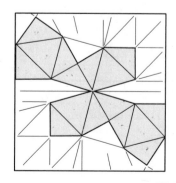

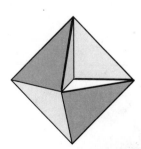

Cubehemioctahedron

Heptahedron

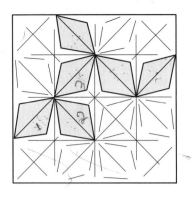
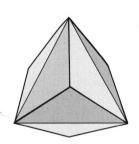
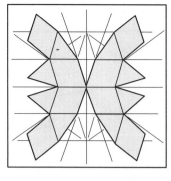

Triakis Tetrahedron

Rhombic Dodecahedron

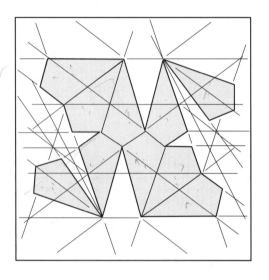
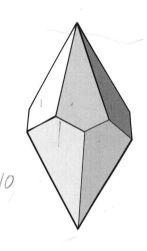

Close up of a quadrilateral:
The small angle is 36°,
the three other angles
are each 108°.

Pentagonal Trapezohedron

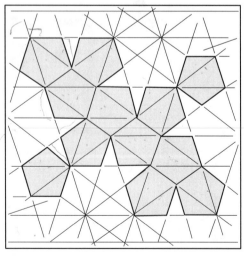
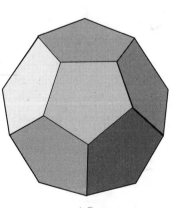
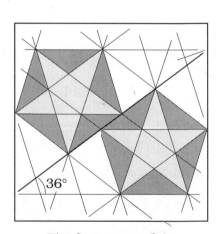

Dodecahedron

The pentagonal trapezohedron and
dodecahedron have the same first
fold. Compare their crease patterns.

The first steps of the
dodecahedron:
1. Fold the 36° line
through the center.
2. Form two pentagons.
3. Form two stars.

Math used for the Dipyramids:

Here is the formula for the angles in the triangles of the of dipyramids which are duals of the uniform prisms with regular polygonal bases and square sides.

These dipyramids are composed of 2n isoceles triangles where n is the number of sides of the polygonal base. Each triangle has angle alpha (α) at the poles and two similar angles beta (β) by the polygon. Note the labeled angles for the hexagonal dipyramid below.

I thank Peter Messer for this information.

Reference:
Peter W. Messer. "Closed-form expressions for uniform polyhedra and their duals". Discrete & Computational Geometry (Springer-Verlag). Forthcoming in 2002.

$$\alpha + 2\beta = 180$$
$$\cos(\alpha) = 1 - 2\sin^4(\pi/n)$$
$$\cos(\beta) = \sin^2(\pi/n)$$

n	$\sin^2(\pi/n)$	α	β
3	0.75	97.18°	41.41°
4	0.5	60.00°	60.00°
5	0.3454915	40.42°	69.79°
6	0.25	28.96°	75.52°
7	0.1882551	21.70°	79.15°

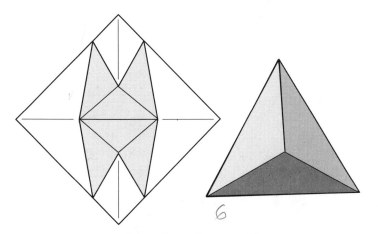

Triangular Dipyramid

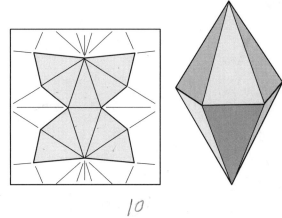

Pentagonal Dipyramid

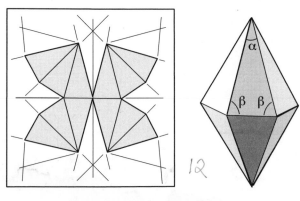

Hexagonal Dipyramid

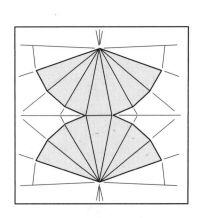

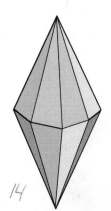

Heptagonal Dipyramid

Afterthoughts

I hope you enjoyed folding these polyhedra.
This use of origami combines art and math
in a beautiful way. I challenge you to create
your own polyhedra using only a single
square sheet for each one. There is still so
much to be discovered and shared.

John Montroll